IT AIN'T OVER 'TIL IT'S OVER

THE WORLD'S GREATEST COLLECTION OF SPORTS QUOTES!

IT AIN'T OVER 'TIL IT'S OVER

THE WORLD'S GREATEST COLLECTION OF SPORTS QUOTES!

JOHN MARLOWE

ARCTURUS

ARCTURUS

This edition published in 2010 by Arcturus Publishing Limited
26/27 Bickels Yard, 151–153 Bermondsey Street,
London SE1 3HA

ISBN: 978-1-84837-452-2
AD001372EN

Printed in China

CONTENTS

INTRODUCTION

On 22 September, 1946, Yogi Berra donned the uniform of the great New York Yankees and took his place on the diamond in his major league debut. His career as a player spanned nearly two decades, during which he became known as one of baseball's greatest catchers and hitters. Later, as a manager, Berra led both the New York Mets and New York Yankees to World Series championships. Nearly half a century after he last played, and two decades since he left coaching, Berra remains a household name. He is recognized by those who have no knowledge of his uncanny ability to hit bad pitches, people for whom the Mets' 1973 season means nothing.

Much of Berra's fame can be attributed not to what he accomplished, but to the words he uttered. 'It ain't over 'til it's over', an observation he made at the darkest point of the 1973 season, is repeated with great regularity by those both inside and outside the game.

As his fame transcends the world of sport, so too do his observations and words of advice. 'You should always go to other people's funerals; otherwise they won't come to yours,' he once cautioned.

While most of the quotes found in this collection originated through experience as an athlete or coach, the best can be applied to everyday life. Here we find words that motivate, inspire and counsel.

The boxer Muhammad Ali is remembered as a great champion – in his own words, 'the greatest'. As an athlete he performed both inside and outside the ring. In interviews, at news conferences and at weigh-ins, Ali was by turns a clown, a comedian, a poet and

★ ★

★ ★

a philosopher. He was almost certainly the most boastful athlete of his day; and yet, when finally meeting with defeat, the man was humble: 'I never thought of losing, but now that it's happened, the only thing is to do it right. That's my obligation to all the people who believe in me. We all have to take defeats in life.'

Many of the most cogent quotes found here come from boxers, golfers, tennis players and others whose skills lie outside the world of team sports. These are, of course, fields of endeavor that encourage introspection and reflection.

Baseball, too, provides similar quotes. Though a team sport, it has at its core two solitary figures, the pitcher and the batter. In the world of athletics, few images convey such a sense of loneliness as those capturing a pitcher on the mound, deep in thought.

The late Warren Zevon wrote of this solitude in his song 'Bill Lee', a tribute to the outspoken, left-handed pitcher for the Boston Red Sox and Montreal Expos. The final line is cut off in mid-sentence: 'Sometimes I say things I shouldn't, like – .'

The example is left up to the listener's imagination… and the choices are many. Unorthodox and unafraid of controversy, Lee said many things that, though true, probably worked against his career prospects.

There are many quotes in this collection that their speakers wish had been left unrecorded. Therefore, it is only fitting that the last word be given to Yogi Berra: 'I never said most of the things I said.'

JOHN MARLOWE
SEPTEMBER 2009
MONTREAL

★ ★

ABILITY AND NATURAL TALENT

'YOU HAVE TO EXPECT THINGS OF YOURSELF BEFORE YOU CAN DO THEM.' **MICHAEL JORDAN** NBA SHOOTING GUARD

'I played the game one way. I gave it everything I had. It doesn't take any ability to hustle.'

WADE BOGGS
MLB THIRD BASEMAN

'Pitchers, like poets, are born not made.'

CY YOUNG
MLB PITCHER

'The five S's of sports training are: stamina, speed, strength, skill and spirit, but the greatest of these is spirit.'

KEN DOHERTY
TRACK AND FIELD ATHLETE

'Ability is what you're capable of doing. Motivation determines what you do. Attitude determines how well you do it.'

LOU HOLTZ
NFL AND COLLEGE FOOTBALL COACH

'God made me fast. And when I run, I feel His pleasure.'

ERIC LIDDELL
TRACK AND FIELD ATHLETE

'To give anything less than your best is to sacrifice the gift.'

STEVE PREFONTAINE
RUNNER

'Then I was skinnier. I hit it better, I putted better, and I could see better. Other than that, everything is the same.'

HOMEO BLANCHAS
GOLFER

'Balanced is probably what I am, although that's just a polite way to say that you don't do anything very well.'

STEVE YZERMAN
NHL CENTER

★ ★

'Baseball and football are very different games. In a way, both of them are easy. Football is easy if you're crazy as hell. Baseball is easy if you've got patience. They'd both be easier for me if I were a little more crazy – and a little more patient.'

BO JACKSON MLB OUTFIELDER AND NFL RUNNING BACK

★ ★

'Do not let what you cannot do interfere with what you can do.'

JOHN WOODEN
COLLEGE BASKETBALL COACH

'Left hand, right hand, it doesn't matter. I'm amphibious.'

CHARLES SHACKLEFORD
NBA FORWARD

'I don't like hockey. I'm just good at it.'

BRETT HULL
NHL RIGHT WINGER

'The uglier a man's legs are, the better he plays golf. It's almost a law.'

H. G. WELLS
NOVELIST AND ESSAYIST

'To be an American and unable to play baseball is comparable to being a Polynesian and unable to swim.'

JOHN CHEEVER
NOVELIST AND SHORT STORY WRITER

'I'm a firm believer in the theory that people only do their best at things they truly enjoy. It is difficult to excel at something you don't enjoy.' **JACK NICKLAUS** GOLFER

★ ★

'In the building I live in on Park Avenue there are ten people who could buy the Yankees, but none of them could hit the ball out of Yankee Stadium.'

REGGIE JACKSON MLB RIGHT FIELDER

★ ★

'You owe it to yourself to be the best you can possibly be – in baseball and in life.'

PETE ROSE
MLB PLAYER AND
MANAGER

'Every game is an opportunity to measure yourself against your own potential.'

BUD WILKINSON
COLLEGE FOOTBALL COACH

'If you can't imitate him, don't copy him.'

YOGI BERRA
MLB PLAYER AND
MANAGER

'Ability is the art of getting credit for all the home runs somebody else hits.'

CASEY STENGEL
MLB OUTFIELDER AND
MANAGER

'Trying to sneak a fastball past Hank Aaron is like trying to sneak the sunrise past a rooster.'

JOE ADCOCK
MLB FIRST BASEMAN

'I am the greatest. I said that even before I knew I was.'

MUHAMMAD ALI
HEAVYWEIGHT BOXER

'You must work very hard to become a natural golfer.'

GARY PLAYER
GOLFER

'The day they put me in the net I had a good game. I've stayed there since.'

TERRY SAWCHUK
NHL GOALIE

'I throw as hard as I can when I think I have to throw as hard as I can.'

WALTER JOHNSON
MLB PITCHER

'Confidence is the most important single factor in this game, and no matter how great your natural talent, there is only one way to obtain and sustain it: work.'

JACK NICKLAUS GOLFER

★ ★

'I looked for the same pitch my whole career, a breaking ball. All of the time. I never worried about the fastball. They couldn't throw it past me, none of them.'

HANK AARON MLB OUTFIELDER

★ ★

'Nobody's a natural. You work hard to get good and then work to get better. It's hard to stay on top.'

PAUL COFFEY
NHL DEFENSEMAN

'I would try and help everybody, because the game was so easy for me. It was just like walking in the park.'

WILLIE MAYS
MLB CENTER FIELDER

'I could never be a manager. All I have is natural ability.'

MICKEY MANTLE
MLB CENTER FIELDER AND FIRST BASEMAN

'All us Youngs could throw. I used to kill squirrels with a stone when I was a kid, and my granddad once killed a turkey buzzard on the fly with a rock.'

CY YOUNG
MLB PITCHER

AGE AND YOUTH

'A MAN WHO VIEWS THE WORLD THE SAME AT FIFTY AS HE DID AT TWENTY HAS WASTED THIRTY YEARS OF HIS LIFE.'
MUHAMMAD ALI HEAVYWEIGHT BOXER

'One of the nice things about the Senior Tour is that we can take a cart and cooler. If your game is not going well, you can always have a picnic.'

LEE TREVINO
GOLFER

'By the time you know what to do, you're too old to do it.'

TED WILLIAMS
MLB LEFTFIELDER

'If you wait, all that happens is that you get older.'

MARIO ANDRETTI
FORMULA 1, INDYCAR AND NASCAR DRIVER

'I feel old when I see mousse in my opponent's hair.'

ANDRE AGASSI
TENNIS PLAYER

'Growing old is mandatory; growing up is optional.'

CHILI DAVIS
MLB OUTFIELDER

'Everyone talks about age, but it's not about age. It's about work ethic. Winning never gets old.'

LISA LESLIE
WNBA CENTER

'Everybody wants to go to heaven, but nobody wants to die.'

JOE LOUIS
HEAVYWEIGHT BOXER

'Baseball was made for kids, and grown-ups only screw it up.'

BOB LEMON
MLB PITCHER AND MANAGER

'Bruce Sutter has been around for a while and he's pretty old. He's thirty-five years old, that will give you some idea of how old he is.'

RON FAIRLY
MLB PLAYER AND BROADCASTER

'Don't force your kids into sports. I never was. To this day, my dad has never asked me to go play golf. I ask him. It's the child's desire to play that matters, not the parent's desire to have the child play. Fun. Keep it fun.'

TIGER WOODS GOLFER

'As years go by, chances of winning here are getting slimmer. That's just a matter of fact.'

STEFAN EDBERG
TENNIS PLAYER

'When I was younger, I was a robot. Wind her up and she plays tennis.'

CHRIS EVERT
TENNIS PLAYER

'I've been in the twilight of my career longer than most people have had their career.'

MARTINA NAVRATILOVA
TENNIS PLAYER

'That's the hard part about sport: as men we haven't started to be in our prime, but as athletes we are old people.'

BORIS BECKER
TENNIS PLAYER

'I'm tired of people questioning me because of my age. If you looked at my numbers and watched me throw and covered my birthdate, would age be an issue?'

RANDY JOHNSON MLB PITCHER

16

★ ★

'Call them pros, call them mercenaries – but in fact they are just grown-up kids who have learned on the frozen creek or flooded corner lot that hockey is the greatest thrill of all.'

LESTER PATRICK NHL DEFENSEMAN

★ ★

'I ain't what I used to be, but who the hell is?'

DIZZY DEAN
MLB PITCHER

'When you get up there in years, the fairways get longer and the holes get smaller.'

BOBBY LOCKE
GOLFER

'You gotta be a man to play baseball for a living, but you gotta have a lot of little boy in you, too.'

ROY CAMPANELLA
MLB CATCHER

'I know we're meant to be these hard-headed, money-obsessed professionals, but we're still little boys at heart. Just ask our wives.'

ROB LEE
SOCCER MIDFIELDER

'Age is a case of mind over matter. If you don't mind, it don't matter.'

SATCHEL PAIGE
MLB PITCHER

'I'm getting so old, I don't even buy green bananas anymore.'

CHI CHI RODRIGUEZ
GOLFER

'I was thinking about making a comeback, until I pulled a muscle vacuuming.'

JOHNNY BENCH
MLB CATCHER

'The older you get, the stronger the wind gets and it's always in your face.'

JACK NICKLAUS
GOLFER

'The older I get, the better I used to be.'

LEE TREVINO
GOLFER

★ ★

'Experience is a great advantage. The problem is that when you get the experience, you're too damned old to do anything about it.'

JIMMY CONNORS TENNIS PLAYER

★ ★

'When you are younger you get blamed for crimes you never committed and when you're older you begin to get credit for virtues you never possessed. It evens itself out.'

CASEY STENGEL MLB OUTFIELDER AND MANAGER

★ ★

'I throw the ball as hard as ever, but it just takes longer to get to the plate.'

DON NEWCOMBE
MLB PITCHER

'Oldtimers weekends and airplane landings are alike. If you can walk away from them, they're successful.'

CASEY STENGEL
MLB OUTFIELDER AND MANAGER

'Jewelry takes people's minds off your wrinkles.'

SONJA HENIE
FIGURE SKATER

'After twelve years, the old butterflies came back. Well, I guess at my age you call them moths.'

FRANCO HARRIS
NFL RUNNING BACK

BRAINS AND BRAWN

'TEAMS DO NOT GO PHYSICALLY FLAT, THEY GO MENTALLY STALE.' **VINCE LOMBARDI** NFL COACH AND GENERAL MANAGER

'Most football players are temperamental. That's 90 percent temper and 10 percent mental.'

DOUG PLANK
NFL SAFETY

'If you don't think too good, don't think too much.'

TED WILLIAMS
MLB LEFTFIELDER

'You don't win tournaments by playing well and thinking poorly.'

LEE WESTWOOD
GOLFER

'Use your brain, not your endurance.'

PETER THOMSON
GOLFER

'Your mind is what makes everything else work.'

KAREEM ABDUL-JABBAR
NBA CENTER

'I'm not comfortable being preachy, but more people need to start spending as much time in the library as they do on the basketball court.'

KAREEM ABDUL-JABBAR
NBA CENTER

'I may be dumb, but I'm not stupid.'

TERRY BRADSHAW
NFL QUARTERBACK AND BROADCASTER

'The doctors X-rayed my head and found nothing.'

DIZZY DEAN
MLB PITCHER

'They always try to play with our minds. But that won't work with our club. We've got twenty guys without brains.'

BOBBY CLARKE
NHL CENTER

'Athletes who take to the classroom naturally or are encouraged to focus on grades should be able to do well in the classroom. I believe the reason you go to college is to get your degree. It's not a minor league or an audition for the pros.'

REBECCA LOBO BASKETBALL CENTER AND BROADCASTER

'Golf is a thinking man's game. You can have all the shots in the bag, but if you don't know what to do with them, you've got troubles.'

CHI CHI RODRIGUEZ
GOLFER

'Competitive golf is played mainly on a five-and-a-half-inch course... the space between your ears.'

BOBBY JONES
GOLFER

'I ain't afraid to tell the world that it didn't take school stuff to help a fella play ball.'

SHOELESS JOE JACKSON
MLB OUTFIELDER

'I don't think genius is a term that applies to football coaches. Geniuses are guys like Norman Einstein.'

JOE THEISMANN
CFL AND NFL QUARTERBACK

'When Brian told me he grew up in New Mexico, I told him I thought it is cool that people from other countries play football. He corrected me on my geography and agreed to sit down with me anyway.'

TERRY BRADSHAW NFL QUARTERBACK AND BROADCASTER

★ ★

'We're not giving away any football players who could hurt us later. I don't mind people thinking I'm stupid, but I don't want to give them any proof.'

BUM PHILLIPS NFL AND COLLEGE FOOTBALL COACH

★ ★

'A light, tender, sensitive touch is worth a ton of brawn.'

PETER THOMSON
GOLFER

'How can you think and hit at the same time?'

YOGI BERRA
MLB PLAYER AND COACH

'I have no trouble with the twelve inches between my elbow and my palm. It's the seven inches between my ears that's bent.'

TUG MCGRAW
MLB PITCHER

'I can do something else besides stuff a ball through a hoop. My biggest resource is my mind.'

KAREEM ABDUL-JABBAR
NBA CENTER

'Concentration is the ability to think about absolutely nothing when it is absolutely necessary.'

RAY KNIGHT
MLB FIRST AND THIRD BASEMAN

'Slow thinkers are part of the game too. Some of these slow thinkers can hit a ball a long way.'

ALVIN DARK
MLB SHORTSTOP AND MANAGER

'I always said you have to be really smart or really dumb to play this game well. I just don't know where I fit in.'

BETH DANIEL
GOLFER

'The difference between winning and losing is always a mental one.'

PETER THOMSON
GOLFER

'When cerebral processes enter into sports, you start screwing up. It's like the Constitution, which says separate church and state. You have to separate mind and body.'

BILL LEE MLB PITCHER

★ ★

'Doctors tell me I have the body of a thirty year old. I know I have the brain of a fifteen year old. If you've got both, you can play baseball.'

PETE ROSE MLB PLAYER AND MANAGER

★ ★

'I was blessed with a strong arm and a weak mind.'

DIZZY DEAN
MLB PITCHER

'Tennis doesn't encourage any kind of intellectual development.'

JIM COURIER
TENNIS PLAYER

'Practice puts brains in your muscles.'

SAM SNEAD
GOLFER

'You can think best when you're happiest.'

PETER THOMSON
GOLFER

'All the time he's boxing, he's thinking. All the time he was thinking, I was hitting him.'

JACK DEMPSEY
HEAVYWEIGHT BOXER

CHALLENGE AND EXPERIENCE

'I'VE HAD TO OVERCOME A LOT OF DIVERSITY.'
DREW GOODEN NBA POWER FORWARD AND CENTER

'Through the years of experience I have found that air offers less resistance than dirt.'

JACK NICKLAUS
GOLFER

'Rather than viewing a brief relapse back to inactivity as a failure, treat it as a challenge and try to get back on track as soon as possible.'

JIMMY CONNORS
TENNIS PLAYER

'When baseball is no longer fun, it's no longer a game.'

JOE DIMAGGIO
MLB CENTER FIELDER

'I don't care how long you've been around, you'll never see it all.'

BOB LEMON
MLB PITCHER AND MANAGER

'Obstacles don't have to stop you. If you run into a wall, don't turn around and give up. Figure out how to climb it, go through it, or work around it.'

MICHAEL JORDAN
NBA SHOOTING GUARD

'Scientists have proven that it's impossible to long-jump 30 feet, but I don't listen to that kind of talk. Thoughts like that have a way of sinking into your feet.'

CARL LEWIS
TRACK AND FIELD ATHLETE

'Experience is a hard teacher because she gives the test first, the lesson afterward.'

VERNON LAW
MLB PITCHER

'The hardest thing I had to overcome in life? I think racism. That's so difficult because I don't think anyone can ever understand it. It's not that people don't want to understand it, but they don't want to touch it.'

HERSCHEL WALKER NFL RUNNING BACK

'Putts get real difficult the day they hand out the money.'

LEE TREVINO
GOLFER

'Life is about obstacles, endeavors in life are not to be overlooked.'

WADE BOGGS
MLB THIRD BASEMAN

'Perhaps the single most important element in mastering the techniques and tactics of racing is experience. But once you have the fundamentals, acquiring the experience is a matter of time.'

GREG LEMOND
CYCLIST

'How can they beat me? I've been struck by lightning, had two back operations, and been divorced twice.'

LEE TREVINO
GOLFER

'I don't run away from a challenge because I am afraid. Instead, I run toward it because the only way to escape fear is to trample it beneath your feet.'

NADIA COMANECI GYMNAST

★ ★

'I'll be sad to go, and I wouldn't be sad to go. It wouldn't upset me to leave St. Louis, but it would upset me to leave St. Louis. It's hard to explain. You'll find out one of these days, but maybe you never will.'

BRETT HULL NHL RIGHT WINGER

★ ★

'The other teams could make trouble for us if they win.'

YOGI BERRA
MLB PLAYER AND MANAGER

'It's lack of faith that makes people afraid of meeting challenges, and I believe in myself.'

MUHAMMAD ALI
HEAVYWEIGHT BOXER

'It's hard not to play golf that's up to Jack Nicklaus standards when you are Jack Nicklaus.'

JACK NICKLAUS
GOLFER

'Winning doesn't always mean being first. Winning means you're doing better than you've ever done before.'

BONNIE BLAIR
SPEEDSKATER

'Golf is a puzzle without an answer. I've played the game for forty years and I still haven't the slightest idea how to play.'

GARY PLAYER
GOLFER

'It's not what you achieve, it's what you overcome. That's what defines your career.'

CARLTON FISK
MLB CATCHER

'The course is going to make you look silly sometimes. You have to be able to accept that and move on.'

MIKE WEIR
GOLFER

'The difference between the impossible and the possible lies in a person's determination.'

TOMMY LASORDA
MLB PITCHER AND MANAGER

'You hear about how many fourth quarter comebacks that a guy has and I think it means a guy screwed up in the first three quarters.'

PEYTON MANNING NFL QUARTERBACK

★ ★

'I have always struggled to achieve excellence. One thing that cycling has taught me is that if you can achieve something without a struggle it's not going to be satisfying.'

GREG LEMOND CYCLIST

★ ★

'I don't care who you are, you hear those boos.'

MICKEY MANTLE
MLB CENTER FIELDER AND FIRST BASEMAN

'Acting is easier than skating in a way and harder in other aspects. In skating, you get one chance, and with acting you get to do it over and over.'

TARA LIPINSKI
FIGURE SKATER

'Becoming number one is easier than remaining number one.'

BILL BRADLEY
MLB THIRD BASEMAN

'It isn't hard to be good from time to time in sports. What is tough is being good every day.'

WILLIE MAYS
MLB CENTER FIELDER

'The word "potential" used to hang over me like a cloud.'

RANDY JOHNSON
MLB PITCHER

'Success depends almost entirely on how effectively you learn to manage the game's two ultimate adversaries: the course and yourself.'

JACK NICKLAUS
GOLFER

'It's hard to beat somebody when they don't give up.'

BABE RUTH
MLB PITCHER AND OUTFIELDER

'Show me someone who has done something worthwhile, and I'll show you someone who has overcome adversity.'

LOU HOLTZ
NFL AND COLLEGE FOOTBALL COACH

★ ★

'How you respond to the challenge in the second half will determine what you become after the game, whether you are a winner or a loser.'

LOU HOLTZ NFL AND COLLEGE FOOTBALL COACH

CHAMPIONS AND CHAMPIONSHIPS

'A CHAMPION IS SOMEONE WHO GETS UP WHEN HE CAN'T.'
JACK DEMPSEY HEAVYWEIGHT BOXER

'Champions keep playing until they get it right.'

BILLIE JEAN KING
TENNIS PLAYER

'If you are going to be a champion, you must be willing to pay a greater price.'

BUD WILKINSON
COLLEGE FOOTBALL COACH

'Heart in champions has to do with the depth of your motivation and how well your mind and body react to pressure.'

BILL RUSSELL
NBA CENTER

'When you are playing for the national championship, it's not a matter of life and death. It's more important than that.'

DUFFY DAUGHERTY
COLLEGE FOOTBALL COACH

'You become a champion by fighting one more round. When things are tough, you fight one more round.'

JAMES J. CORBETT
HEAVYWEIGHT BOXER

'Being champion is all well and good, but you can't eat a crown.'

ALTHEA GIBSON
TENNIS PLAYER

'I had always dreamed of winning Wimbledon and when it happened it was very stressful. It was more of a relief!'

PAT CASH
TENNIS PLAYER

'Just give me 25 guys on the last year of their contracts; I'll win a pennant every year.'

SPARKY ANDERSON
MLB MANAGER

★ ★

'I have to consider my greatest accomplishment's winning the Olympics because everything that I've done after that is really because of the Olympics.'

BRIAN BOITANO FIGURE SKATER

★ ★

'The reason sport is attractive to many of the general public is that it's filled with reversals. What you think may happen doesn't happen. A champion is beaten, an unknown becomes a champion.'

ROGER BANNISTER RUNNER

★ ★

'Where do you go when you're the best in the world? What's next?'

BORIS BECKER
TENNIS PLAYER

'True champions aren't always the ones that win, but those with the most guts.'

MIA HAMM
SOCCER PLAYER

'What could be better than walking down any street in any city and knowing you're the heavyweight champion of the world?'

ROCKY MARCIANO
HEAVYWEIGHT BOXER

'Gold medals aren't really made of gold. They're made of sweat, determination, and a hard-to-find alloy called guts.'

DAN GABLE
OLYMPIC WRESTLER

'I'll put you through hell, but at the end of it all we'll be champions.'

BEAR BRYANT
football coach

'A trophy carries dust. Memories last forever.'

MARY LOU RETTON
GYMNAST

'You can be the best person in the league, but if you don't win championships, something's missing.'

TERRELL DAVIS
NFL RUNNING BACK

'I think to compare any time you win a Stanley Cup would be unfair to all the players from all the teams.'

MARK MESSIER
NHL CENTER

★ ★

'Part of being a champ is acting like a champ. You have to learn how to win and not run away when you lose. Everyone has bad stretches and real successes. Either way, you have to be careful not to lose your confidence or get too confident.'

NANCY KERRIGAN FIGURE SKATER

★ ★

'I don't think a manager should be judged by whether he wins the pennant, but by whether he gets the most out of the twenty-five men he's been given.'

CHUCK TANNER MLB OUTFIELDER AND MANAGER

★ ★

'It's hard to win a pennant, but it's harder to lose one.'

CHUCK TANNER
MLB OUTFIELDER AND
MANAGER

'You know what a champion is? A champion is someone who's ready when the gong rings – not just before, not just after – but when it rings.'

JACK DEMPSEY
HEAVYWEIGHT BOXER

'A champion owes everybody something. He can never pay back for all the help he got, for making him an idol.'

JACK DEMPSEY
HEAVYWEIGHT BOXER

'I've won at every level, except college and pro.'

SHAQUILLE O'NEAL
NBA CENTER

'I'd run over my mother to win the Super Bowl.'

JOE JACOBY
NFL OFFENSIVE TACKLE

'If you get depressed about being the second-best team in the world, then you've got a problem.'

JULIUS ERVING
ABA AND NBA SMALL FORWARD

'The only yardstick for success our society has is being a champion. No one remembers anything else.'

JOHN MADDEN
NFL COACH AND COMMENTATOR

'I haven't celebrated coming in Number Two too many times.'

MARK MESSIER
NHL CENTER

★ ★

'In sports, you simply aren't considered a real champion until you have defended your title successfully. Winning it once can be a fluke; winning it twice proves you are the best.'

ALTHEA GIBSON TENNIS PLAYER

★ ★

'The only thing bad about winning the pennant is that you have to manage the All-Star Game the next year. I'd rather go fishing for three years.'

WHITEY HERZOG MLB OUTFIELDER AND MANAGER

★ ★

'I cried a little bit in the race car on the way to the checkered flag. Well, maybe not cried, but at least my eyes watered up.'

DALE EARNHARDT, JR.
NASCAR DRIVER

'I didn't aspire to be a good sport; "champion" was good enough for me.'

FRED PERRY
TENNIS PLAYER

'The Internal Revenue Service is the real undefeated heavyweight champion.'

GEORGE FOREMAN
HEAVYWEIGHT BOXER

CHARACTER AND CONFIDENCE

'SPORTS DO NOT BUILD CHARACTER. THEY REVEAL IT.'
HEYWOOD HALE BROWN SPORTSWRITER AND COMMENTATOR

'There are some people who, if they don't already know, you can't tell 'em.'

YOGI BERRA
MLB PLAYER AND COACH

'I am many things. I am an animal. I am a convicted rapist, a hell-raiser, a loving father, a semi-good husband. You don't really know me.'

MIKE TYSON
HEAVYWEIGHT BOXER

'A kid grows up a lot faster on the golf course. Golf teaches you how to behave.'

JACK NICKLAUS
GOLFER

'I'm just a dark guy from a den of iniquity. A dark shadowy figure from the bowels of iniquity.'

MIKE TYSON
HEAVYWEIGHT BOXER

'They say some of my stars drink whiskey, but I have found that ones who drink milkshakes don't win many ball games.'

CASEY STENGEL
MLB OUTFIELDER AND MANAGER

'I keep telling myself, don't get cocky. Give your services to the press and the media, be nice to the kids, throw a baseball into the stands once in a while.'

VIDA BLUE
MLB PITCHER

'There's no such thing as lack of confidence. You either have it or you don't.'

ROB ANDREW
RUGBY PLAYER

'Only a man who knows what it is like to be defeated can reach down to the bottom of his soul and come up with the extra ounce of power it takes to win when the match is even.'

MUHAMMAD ALI HEAVYWEIGHT BOXER

'Awards mean a lot, but they don't say it all. The people in baseball mean more to me than statistics.'

ERNIE BANKS
MLB SHORTSTOP AND FIRST BASEMAN

'A wise person decides slowly but abides by these decisions.'

ARTHUR ASHE
TENNIS PLAYER

'You learn you can do your best when it's hard, even when you're tired and maybe hurting a little bit. It feels good to show some courage.'

JOE NAMATH
NFL QUARTERBACK

'When they treat you bad, you just got to take care of your pride, no matter what.'

SATCHEL PAIGE
MLB PITCHER

'Developing better people should be the number one goal for any coach when dealing with kids. In trying to develop better people, we are going to develop more and better pros.'

BOBBY ORR NHL DEFENSEMAN

★ ★

'You can ask anybody in the room. My numbers are the worst in here, but I'm still a jerk to everybody, yelling at everybody, getting them going. Once I get it back, then I'll be even worse to the guys.'

BILLY KOCH MLB PITCHER

★ ★

'A positive attitude causes a chain reaction of positive thoughts, events and outcomes. It is a catalyst and it sparks extraordinary results.'

WADE BOGGS
MLB THIRD BASEMAN

'I always try to act as though there is a little boy or a little girl around, and I try never to do anything that would give them a bad example.'

STEVE GARVEY
MLB FIRST BASEMAN

'I never did say that you can't be a nice guy and win. I said that if I was playing third base and my mother rounded third with the winning run, I'd trip her up.'

LEO DUROCHER
MLB SHORTSTOP AND MANAGER

43

'Why is it there are so many nice guys interested in baseball? Not me, I was a real bastard when I played.'

BURLEIGH GRIMES
MLB PITCHER

'I became an optimist when I discovered that I wasn't going to win any more games by being anything else.'

EARL WEAVER
MLB MANAGER

'Everything negative – pressure, challenges – is all an opportunity for me to rise.'

KOBE BRYANT
NBA SHOOTING GUARD

'This whole thing's about development. Not only are we trying to develop players, we're trying to develop ourselves.'

MICHAEL COOPER
NBA PLAYER AND WNBA COACH

'Not to be cheered by praise, not to be grieved by blame, but to know thoroughly one's own virtues or powers are the characteristics of an excellent man.'

SATCHEL PAIGE MLB PITCHER

★ ★

'I have the same malice in my heart as far as the fight game is concerned, but outside the ring, I won't say anything a dignified man won't say.'

MIKE TYSON HEAVYWEIGHT BOXER

★ ★

'I may have been fierce, but never low or underhand.'

TY COBB
MLB OUTFIELDER

'When you go out there and do the things you're supposed to do, people view you as selfish.'

WILT CHAMBERLAIN
NBA CENTER

'I was introverted, shy. But if you win a lot you need to be extroverted, or they'll think you're arrogant.'

ALBERTO TOMBA
SKIER

'I've always believed that you can think positive just as well as you can think negative.'

SUGAR RAY ROBINSON
BOXER

45

'My biggest weakness is my sensitivity. I am too sensitive a person.'

MIKE TYSON
HEAVYWEIGHT BOXER

'Clothes and manners do not make the man; but when he is made, they greatly improve his appearance.'

ARTHUR ASHE
TENNIS PLAYER

'I think it's the mark of a great player to be confident in tough situations.'

JOHN MCENROE
TENNIS PLAYER

'Stroke play is a better test of golf, but match play is a better test of character.'

JOE CARR
GOLFER

'Be more concerned with your character than with your reputation. Your character is what you really are while your reputation is merely what others think you are.'

JOHN WOODEN COLLEGE BASKETBALL COACH

COACHES AND COACHING

'ON THIS TEAM, WE'RE ALL UNITED IN A COMMON GOAL: TO KEEP MY JOB.' **LOU HOLTZ** NFL AND COLLEGE FOOTBALL COACH

'All managers are losers, they are the most expendable pieces of furniture on the face of the Earth.'

TED WILLIAMS
MLB LEFTFIELDER

'We can't win at home and we can't win on the road. My problem as general manager is I can't think of another place to play.'

PAT WILLIAMS
NBA MANAGER

'If history is going to repeat itself I should think we can expect the same thing again.'

TERRY VENABLES
SOCCER PLAYER AND MANAGER

'Even Jesus had trouble with twelve guys.'

FRANK LAYDEN
NBA COACH

'It was important to me to believe, because if I don't believe, how can I expect them to believe?'

ISIAH THOMAS
NBA POINT GUARD AND COACH

'I wouldn't say I was the best manager in the business. But I was in the top one.'

BRIAN CLOUGH
SOCCER STRIKER AND MANAGER

'If you don't win, you're going to be fired. If you do win, you've only put off the day you're going to be fired.'

LEO DUROCHER
MLB SHORTSTOP AND MANAGER

'The secret of managing is to keep the guys who hate you away from the guys who are undecided.'

CASEY STENGEL
MLB OUTFIELDER AND MANAGER

'If anything goes bad, I did it. If anything goes semi-good, then we did it. If anything goes really good, then you did it. That's all it takes to get people to win football games.'

BEAR BRYANT COLLEGE FOOTBALL COACH

★ ★

'Some players you pat their butts, some players you
kick their butts, some players you leave alone.'

PETE ROSE MLB PLAYER AND MANAGER

★ ★

*'Show me a good sportsman
and I'll show you a player I'm
looking to trade.'*

LEO DUROCHER
MLB SHORTSTOP AND
MANAGER

*'I'm not buddy-buddy
with the players. If they need
a buddy, let them
buy a dog.'*

WHITEY HERZOG
MLB OUTFIELDER AND
MANAGER

*'The worst thing is the day
you realize you want to win
more than the players do.'*

GENE MAUCH
MLB SECOND BASEMAN AND
MANAGER

*'The country
is full of
good
coaches.
What it
takes to win
is a bunch of
interested
players.'*

DON CORYELL
NFL COACH

'I'm not the manager because I'm always right, but I'm always right because I'm the manager.'

GENE MAUCH
MLB SECOND BASEMAN
AND MANAGER

'They say you're not a coach in the league till you've been fired. I must be getting pretty good.'

TERRY SIMPSON
NHL COACH

'You don't save a pitcher for tomorrow. Tomorrow it may rain.'

LEO DUROCHER
MLB SHORTSTOP AND
MANAGER

'In a crisis, don't hide behind anything or anybody. They are going to find you anyway.'

BEAR BRYANT
COLLEGE
FOOTBALL COACH

'If you make every game a life and death proposition, you're going to have problems. For one thing, you'll be dead a lot.'

DEAN SMITH COLLEGE BASKETBALL COACH

★ ★

'I'd rather be a football coach. That way you can lose only eleven games a season. I lost eleven games in December alone.'

ABE LEMONS COLLEGE BASKETBALL COACH

★ ★

'Trade a player a year too early rather than a year too late.'

BRANCH RICKEY
MLB CATCHER AND MANAGER

'The way we're going, if I called up another pitcher, he'd just hang up the phone on me.'

FRANK ROBINSON
MLB OUTFIELDER AND MANAGER

'A manager doesn't hear the cheers.'

ALVIN DARK
MLB SHORTSTOP AND MANAGER

'Coaching is nothing more than eliminating mistakes before you get fired.'

LOU HOLTZ
NFL AND COLLEGE FOOTBALL COACH

51

'I'm the football coach around here and don't you remember it.'

BILL PETERSON
COLLEGE FOOTBALL COACH

'I learn teaching from teachers. I learn golf from golfers. I learn winning from coaches.'

HARVEY PENICK
GOLFER

'Make sure that team members know they are working with you, not for you.'

JOHN WOODEN
COLLEGE BASKETBALL COACH

'Coaching is easy. Winning is the hard part.'

ELGIN BAYLOR
NBA FORWARD AND GENERAL MANAGER

'If you're playing baseball and thinking about managing, you're crazy. You'd be better off thinking about being an owner.'

CASEY STENGEL MLB OUTFIELDER AND MANAGER

★ ★

'They say Yogi Berra is funny. Well, he has a lovely wife and family, a beautiful home, money in the bank, and he plays golf with millionaires. What's funny about that?'

CASEY STENGEL MLB OUTFIELDER AND MANAGER

★ ★

'Half the lies they tell about me aren't true.'

YOGI BERRA
MLB PLAYER AND MANAGER

'Yogi seemed to be doing everything wrong, yet everything came out right.'

MEL OTT
MLB RIGHT FIELDER

'There is nothing so uncertain as a sure thing.'

SCOTTY BOWMAN
NHL COACH

'You get the best effort from others not by lighting a fire beneath them, but by building a fire within.'

BOB NELSON
FOOTBALLER

53

CRITICISM AND COMPLAINTS

'NO ONE WANTS TO HEAR ABOUT THE LABOR PAINS, THEY JUST WANT TO SEE THE BABY.' **LOU BROCK** MLB LEFT FIELDER

'Some people are born on third base and go through life thinking they hit a triple.'

BARRY SWITZER
NFL COACH

'I don't care where you are, but the fans only remember your last time at bat.'

MIKE DITKA
NFL TIGHT END AND COACH

'When my time on earth is gone, and my activities here are passed, I want they bury me upside down, and my critics can kiss my ass!'

BOBBY KNIGHT
COLLEGE BASKETBALL COACH

'The day you hear someone call me captain will be the day I buy a boat.'

GUY LAFLEUR
NHL RIGHT WINGER

'Rail-splitting produced an immortal president in Lincoln, but golf hasn't produced even a good Congressman.'

WILL ROGERS
ACTOR AND HUMORIST

'That's my gift. I let that negativity roll off me like water off a duck's back. If it's not positive, I didn't hear it. If you can overcome that, fights are easy.'

GEORGE FOREMAN
HEAVYWEIGHT BOXER

'Baseball has the great advantage over cricket of being sooner ended.'

GEORGE BERNARD SHAW
PLAYWRIGHT AND ESSAYIST

'I know that I'm never as good or bad as any single performance. I've never believed my critics or my worshippers, and I've always been able to leave the game at the arena.'

CHARLES BARKLEY NBA FORWARD

'The great trouble with baseball today is that most of the players are in the game for the money and that's it, not for the love of it, the excitement of it, the thrill of it.'

TY COBB
MLB OUTFIELDER

'Every sport pretends to a literature, but people don't believe it of any other sport but their own.'

ALISTAIR COOKE
JOURNALIST AND BROADCASTER

'Baseball must be a great game to survive the fools who run it.'

BILL TERRY
MLB FIRST BASEMAN

'If the NBA were on channel 5 and a bunch of frogs making love were on channel 4, I'd watch the frogs, even if they were coming in fuzzy.'

BOBBY KNIGHT
COLLEGE BASKETBALL COACH

'The difference between the old ballplayer and the new ballplayer is the jersey. The old ballplayer cared about the name on the front. The new ballplayer cares about the name on the back.'

STEVE GARVEY MLB FIRST BASEMAN

★ ★

'Serious sport has nothing to do with fair play. It is bound up with hatred, jealousy, boastfulness, disregard of all rules and sadistic pleasure in witnessing violence. In other words, it is war minus the shooting.'

GEORGE ORWELL NOVELIST AND ESSAYIST

★ ★

'The game has a cleanness. If you do a good job, the numbers say so. You don't have to ask anyone or play politics. You don't have to wait for the reviews.'

SANDY KOUFAX
MLB PITCHER

'When a man wantonly destroys one of the works of man we call him a vandal, when he wantonly destroys one of the works of God we call him a sportsman.'

JOSEPH WOOD KRUTCH
CRITIC AND NATURALIST

'My family got all over me because they said Bush is only for the rich people. Then I reminded them, "Hey, I'm rich."'

CHARLES BARKLEY
NBA POWER FORWARD

'80 percent
of the
top 100
women are
fat pigs
who don't
deserve
equal pay.'

RICHARD KRAJICEK
TENNIS PLAYER

'If you don't like the way
the Atlanta Braves are
playing then you don't
like baseball.'

CHUCK TANNER
MLB OUTFIELDER AND
MANAGER

'Baseball is what we were,
football is what we have
become.'

MARY MᶜGRORY
COLUMNIST

'Two hundred million
Americans, and there
ain't two good catchers
among 'em.'

CASEY STENGEL
MLB OUTFIELDER AND
MANAGER

★ ★

'If I had my way no man guilty of golf would be eligible
to any office of trust under the United States.'

H. L. MENCKEN CRITIC AND ESSAYIST

★ ★

'You don't think people would go on about my looks if I was Number 500 in the world instead of Number 12, do you? Anyway, as I keep telling everyone, you can't blame me for looking like this on purpose.'

ANNA KOURNIKOVA TENNIS PLAYER

★ ★

'I was a lousy hitter in May doing the same things that made me a great hitter in June.'

CARL YASTRZEMSKI
MLB LEFT FIELDER AND FIRST BASEMAN

'Don't ever forget two things I'm going to tell you. One, don't believe everything that's written about you. Two, don't pick up too many checks.'

BABE RUTH
MLB PITCHER AND OUTFIELDER

'Why does everybody stand up and sing "Take Me Out to the Ballgame" when they're already there?'

LARRY ANDERSON
MLB PITCHER

'The only way to shut everybody up is to win.'

TERRY BRADSHAW
BROADCASTER AND
NFL QUARTERBACK

'Games played with the ball, and others of that nature, are too violent for the body and stamp no character on the mind.'

THOMAS JEFFERSON
UNITED STATES
PRESIDENT

'Difficulties in life are intended to make us better, not bitter.'

DAN REEVES
NFL RUNNING BACK
AND COACH

'When we played, World Series checks meant something. Now all they do is screw up your taxes.'

DON DRYSDALE
MLB PITCHER

★ ★

'Some people asked me if I would be interested in managing the A's. I said a definite no thank you. At night, that place is a graveyard with lights.'

WHITEY HERZOG MLB OUTFIELDER AND MANAGER

★ ★

'There's nothing masculine about being competitive. There's nothing masculine about trying to be the best at everything you do, nor is there anything wrong with it. I don't know why a female athlete has to defend her femininity just because she chooses to play sports.'

REBECCA LOBO BASKETBALL CENTER AND BROADCASTER

★ ★

'Joe Frazier is so ugly he should donate his face to the US Bureau of Wildlife.'

MUHAMMAD ALI
HEAVYWEIGHT BOXER

'I'm not the next [Anna] Kournikova — I want to win matches.'

MARIA SHARAPOVA
TENNIS PLAYER

'What I said to the team at half-time would be unprintable on the radio.'

GERRY FRANCIS
SOCCER COACH

'The trouble with baseball is that it is not played the year round.'

GAYLORD PERRY
MLB PITCHER

DREAMS AND GOALS

'CHAMPIONS AREN'T MADE IN THE GYMS. CHAMPIONS ARE MADE FROM SOMETHING THEY HAVE DEEP INSIDE THEM: A DESIRE, A DREAM, A VISION.' **MUHAMMAD ALI** HEAVYWEIGHT BOXER

'Be a dreamer. If you don't know how to dream, you're dead.'

JIM VALVANO
COLLEGE BASKETBALL COACH

'Twenty-five years later, you know, I haven't really put too much emphasis on any kind of individual goal, other than trying to win any particular night, trying to find a way to do that.'

MARK MESSIER
NHL CENTER

'It was one of those goals that's invariably a goal.'

DENIS LAW
SOCCER CENTER FORWARD

'You can't put a limit on anything. The more you dream, the farther you get.'

MICHAEL PHELPS
SWIMMER

'I had dreams of catching the ball for the final out in the World Series and being mobbed by my teammates. Well, I guess all my dreams didn't come true.'

ROBIN YOUNT
MLB SHORTSTOP AND
CENTER FIELDER

'I think about baseball when I wake up in the morning. I think about it all day and I dream about it at night. The only time I don't think about it is when I'm playing it.'

CARL YASTRZEMSKI
MLB LEFT FIELDER AND FIRST
BASEMAN

'I want to be what I've always wanted to be: dominant.'

TIGER WOODS
GOLFER

'You can't climb up to the second floor without a ladder. When you set your aim too high and don't fulfill it, then your enthusiasm turns to bitterness. Try for a goal that's reasonable, and then gradually raise it.'

EMIL ZATOPEK RUNNER

'When I was young, I never wanted to leave the court until I got things exactly correct. My dream was to become a pro.'

LARRY BIRD
NBA FORWARD

'The baseball field was my fantasy of what life offered.'

LOU BROCK
MLB LEFT FIELDER

'My goal is the same as every year – to not hurt myself.'

BODE MILLER
SKIER

'I want to rush for 1,000 or 1,500 yards, whichever comes first.'

GEORGE ROGERS
NFL RUNNING BACK

'The sportsman knows that a sport is a recreation, a game, an amusement and a pastime, but his eyes are fixed on a higher goal, on the most important thing in his life, which is his education or his vocation.'

AVERY BRUNDAGE TRACK AND FIELD ATHLETE

★ ★

'No matter how good you are, you're going to lose one-third of your games. No matter how bad you are you're going to win one-third of your games. It's the other third that makes the difference.'

TOMMY LASORDA MLB PITCHER AND MANAGER

★ ★

'I just want to conquer people and their souls.'

MIKE TYSON
HEAVYWEIGHT BOXER

'I wanted to be Gene Kelly. Well really, I just wanted to dance with Cyd Charisse.'

ROBIN COUSINS
FIGURE SKATER

'Winners, I am convinced, imagine their dreams first. They want it with all their heart and expect it to come true.'

JOE MONTANA
NFL QUARTERBACK

'An athlete cannot run with money in his pockets. He must run with hope in his heart and dreams in his head.'

EMIL ZATOPEK
RUNNER

'You shoot for the stars. Sometimes you only make it to the moon.'

ADAM VAN KOEVERDEN
KAYAKER

'Set your goals high, and don't stop till you get there.'

BO JACKSON
MLB OUTFIELDER AND NFL RUNNING BACK

'Forget goals. Value the process.'

JIM BOUTON
MLB PITCHER

'Goals determine what you're going to be.'

JULIUS ERVING
NBA FORWARD

'Nobody but the world's top-ranked player knows what it takes to get to the top. You have to sacrifice everything.'

BJORN BORG
TENNIS PLAYER

★ ★

'There is nothing wrong with dedication and goals, but if you focus on yourself, all the lights fade away and you become a fleeting moment in life.'

PETE MARAVICH NBA GUARD

★ ★

'Basketball, hockey and track meets are action heaped upon action, climax upon climax, until the onlooker's responses become deadened. Baseball is for the leisurely afternoons of summer and for the unchanging dreams.'

ROGER KAHN SPORTSWRITER

★ ★

'I'm a dreamer. I have to dream and reach for the stars, and if I miss a star then I grab a handful of clouds.'

MIKE TYSON
HEAVYWEIGHT BOXER

'I tell kids to pursue their basketball dreams, but I tell them to not let that be their only dream.'

KAREEM ABDUL-JABBAR
NBA CENTER

'You have to dream dreams to live dreams.'

ERIC LINDROS
NHL CENTER

'We're going to turn this team around 360 degrees.'

JASON KIDD
NBA POINT GUARD

EGO AND PRIDE

'I PLAY GOLF WITH FRIENDS SOMETIMES, BUT THERE
ARE NEVER FRIENDLY GAMES.'
BEN HOGAN GOLFER

'I'm not the greatest; I'm the double greatest. Not only do I knock 'em out, I pick the round.'

MUHAMMAD ALI
HEAVYWEIGHT BOXER

'I didn't come to New York to be a star, I brought my star with me.'

REGGIE JACKSON
MLB PITCHER

'I'm a competitor and a very proud man. If a guy beats me once, he'll have to do it again to make me believe him.'

SUGAR RAY LEONARD
WELTERWEIGHT BOXER

'I'm so fast that last night I turned off the light switch in my hotel room and was in bed before the room was dark.'

MUHAMMAD ALI
HEAVYWEIGHT BOXER

'My performances have finally caught up with my ego.'

ATO BOLDON
TRACK AND FIELD ATHLETE

'I really lack the words to compliment myself today.'

ALBERTO TOMBA
SKIER

'At home I am a nice guy, but I don't want the world to know. Humble people, I've found, don't get very far.'

MUHAMMAD ALI
HEAVYWEIGHT BOXER

'Anybody who's ever had the privilege of seeing me play knows that I am the greatest pitcher in the world.'

DIZZY DEAN
MLB PITCHER

'There is a difference between conceit and confidence. Conceit is bragging about yourself. Confidence means you believe you can get the job done.'

JOHNNY UNITAS NFL QUARTERBACK

'You'll never catch me bragging about goals, but I'll talk all you want about my assists.'

WAYNE GRETZKY
NHL CENTER

'The only reason I don't like playing in the World Series is I can't watch myself play.'

REGGIE JACKSON
MLB PITCHER

'I know fear is an obstacle for some people, but it's an illusion to me.'

MICHAEL JORDAN
NBA SHOOTING GUARD

'I could feel his muscle tissues collapse under my force. It's ludicrous these mortals even attempt to enter my realm.'

MIKE TYSON
HEAVYWEIGHT BOXER

★ ★

'I am the astronaut of boxing. Joe Louis and Dempsey were just jet pilots. I'm in a world of my own.'

MUHAMMAD ALI HEAVYWEIGHT BOXER

★ ★

'George Foreman. A miracle. A mystery to myself. Who am I? The mirror says back. The George you was always meant to be. Wasn't always like that. Used to look in the mirror and cried a river.'

GEORGE FOREMAN HEAVYWEIGHT BOXER

★ ★

'I'll always be Number One to myself.'

MOSES MALONE
ABA AND NBA CENTER
AND POWER FORWARD

'The more self-centered and egotistical a guy is, the better ballplayer he's going to be.'

BILL LEE
MLB PITCHER

'I'm not God – but I am something similar.'

ROBERTO DURAN
LIGHTWEIGHT BOXER

'I feel like I'm the best, but you're not going to get me to say that.'

JERRY RICE
NFL WIDE RECEIVER

'Somebody may beat me, but they are going to have to bleed to do it.'

STEVE PREFONTAINE
RUNNER

'These young guys are playing checkers. I'm out there playing chess.'

KOBE BRYANT
NBA SHOOTING GUARD

'I think I was the best baseball player I ever saw.'

WILLIE MAYS
MLB CENTER FIELDER

'All I'm asking for is what I want.'

RICKEY HENDERSON
MLB LEFT FIELDER

'I have a lot to say, and if I'm not Number One, I can't say it.'

BILLIE JEAN KING
TENNIS PLAYER

★ ★

'I think I have the best swing on the tour. Why have scores come down in the last ten years? Partly because they are imitating me.'

LEE TREVINO GOLFER

★ ★

'On occasions I have been big-headed. I think most people are when they get in the limelight. I call myself Big Head just to remind myself not to be.'

BRIAN CLOUGH SOCCER PLAYER AND MANAGER

★ ★

'I was such a dangerous hitter I even got intentional walks in batting practice.'

CASEY STENGEL
MLB OUTFIELDER AND MANAGER

'I don't create controversies. They're there long before I open my mouth. I just bring them to your attention.'

CHARLES BARKLEY
NBA FORWARD

'I don't like to sound egotistical, but every time I stepped up to the plate with a bat in my hands, I couldn't help but feel sorry for the pitcher.'

ROGERS HORNSBY
MLB SECOND BASEMAN
AND MANAGER

'I don't really care what the man on the street thinks. I never did anything to please him in the first place, and I'm not going to start now.'

BORIS BECKER
TENNIS PLAYER

EXCUSES AND EXPLANATIONS

'WE DIDN'T LOSE THE GAME; WE JUST RAN OUT OF TIME.'
VINCE LOMBARDI NFL COACH AND GENERAL MANAGER

'The man who complains about the way the ball bounces is likely to be the one who dropped it.'

LOU HOLTZ
NFL AND COLLEGE FOOTBALL COACH

'You wouldn't have won if we'd beaten you.'

YOGI BERRA
MLB PLAYER AND MANAGER

'Hell, if I didn't drink or smoke, I'd win twenty games every year. It's easy when you don't drink or smoke or horse around.'

WHITEY FORD
MLB PITCHER

'The only thing that keeps this organization from being recognized as one of the finest in baseball is wins and losses at the major league level.'

CHUCK LAMAR
MLB GENERAL MANAGER

*'Everything in our favor
was against us.'*

**DANNY
BLANCHFLOWER**
SOCCER MIDFIELDER,
COACH AND JOURNALIST

*'If you're not balanced,
your mind's
not balanced...
my fuse went.'*

FRANK BRUNO
HEAVYWEIGHT BOXER

*'I always mean what I
say, but I don't always
say what I'm thinking.'*

DEAN SMITH
COLLEGE BASKETBALL
COACH

'Sports are
the reason
I am out
of shape.
I watch
them all
on TV.'

THOMAS SOWELL
ECONOMIST AND COMMENTATOR

'The most cowardly thing in the world is blaming mistakes upon
the umpires. Too many managers strut around on the field trying
to manage the umpires instead of their teams.'

BILL KLEM MLB UMPIRE

'I don't care what the tape says. I didn't say it.'

RAY MALAVASI
NFL COACH

'Sometimes that light at the end of the tunnel is a train.'

CHARLES BARKLEY
NBA POWER FORWARD

'I could have been a Rhodes Scholar, except for my grades.'

DUFFY DAUGHERTY
COLLEGE FOOTBALL COACH

'The more I practice, the luckier I get.'

GARY PLAYER
GOLFER

'You argue with the umpire because there is nothing else you can do about it.'

LEO DUROCHER
MLB SHORTSTOP
AND MANAGER

'The last time the Cubs won a World Series was in 1908. The last time they were in one was 1945. Hey, any team can have a bad century.'

TOM TREBELHORN MLB MANAGER

★ ★

'I never blame myself when I'm not hitting. I just blame the bat and if it keeps up, I change bats. After all, if I know it isn't my fault that I'm not hitting, how can I get mad at myself?'

YOGI BERRA MLB PLAYER AND MANAGER

★ ★

'Now there's three things you can do in a baseball game: you can win or you can lose or it can rain.'

CASEY STENGEL
MLB OUTFIELDER AND MANAGER

'Tennis is a psychological sport; you have to keep a clear head. That is why I stopped playing.'

BORIS BECKER
TENNIS PLAYER

'That's why I don't talk. Because I talk too much.'

JOAQUIN ANDUJAR
MLB PITCHER

'I don't think of myself as giving interviews. I just have conversations. That gets me in trouble.'

CHARLES BARKLEY
NBA POWER FORWARD

'Pressure, that's something you feel when you don't know what the hell you're doing.'

PEYTON MANNING
NFL QUARTERBACK

'Sometimes they write what I say and not what I mean.'

PEDRO GUERRERO
MLB INFIELDER AND OUTFIELDER

'Slump? I ain't in no slump... I just ain't hitting.'

YOGI BERRA
MLB PLAYER AND MANAGER

'Luck is the great stabilizer in baseball.'

TRIS SPEAKER
MLB OUTFIELDER AND MANAGER

'Once a guy starts wearing silk pajamas, it's hard to get up early.'

EDDIE ARCARO
JOCKEY

★ ★

'We have a great bunch of outside shooters. Unfortunately, all our games are played indoors.'

WELDON DREW COLLEGE BASKETBALL COACH

★ ★

'As soon as I step on the court I just try to play tennis and don't find excuses. You know, I just lost because I lost, not because my arm was sore.'

GORAN IVANISEVIC TENNIS PLAYER

★ ★

'It is easier to do a job right than to explain why you didn't.'

MARTINA NAVRATILOVA
TENNIS PLAYER

'I never said most of the things I said.'

YOGI BERRA
MLB PLAYER AND MANAGER

'Good luck is a residue of preparation.'

JACK YOUNGBLOOD
NFL DEFENSIVE END

'I didn't play the game right because I saw a reward at the end of the tunnel.'

RYNE SANDBERG
MLB SECOND BASEMAN

'Being with a woman all night never hurt no professional baseball player. It's staying up all night looking for a woman that does him in.'

CASEY STENGEL
MLB OUTFIELDER
AND MANAGER

FAILURE AND MISTAKES

'I ALWAYS TURN TO THE SPORTS PAGES FIRST, WHICH RECORDS PEOPLE'S ACCOMPLISHMENTS. THE FRONT PAGE HAS NOTHING BUT MAN'S FAILURES.'

EARL WARREN CHIEF JUSTICE OF THE UNITED STATES

'Slumps are like a soft bed. They're easy to get into and hard to get out of.'

JOHNNY BENCH
MLB CATCHER

'Success isn't permanent and failure isn't fatal.'

MIKE DITKA
NFL PLAYER AND COACH

'I decided I can't pay a person to rewind time, so I may as well get over it.'

SERENA WILLIAMS
TENNIS PLAYER

'At 49, I can say something I never would have said when I was a player, that I'm a better person because of my failures and disgraces.'

BILL WALTON
NBA CENTER

80

'Life is very interesting if you make mistakes.'

GEORGES CARPENTIER
BOXER

'We were so bad last year, the cheerleaders stayed home and phoned in the cheers.'

PAT WILLIAMS
NBA MANAGER

'Some people are so busy learning the tricks of the trade that they never learn the trade.'

VERNON LAW
MLB PITCHER

'Every season has peaks and valleys. You have to try to eliminate the Grand Canyon.'

ANDY VAN SLYKE
MLB OUTFIELDER AND COACH

★ ★

'You can't be afraid to make errors. You can't be afraid to be naked before the crowd, because no one can ever master the game of baseball, or conquer it. You can only challenge it.'

LOU BROCK MLB LEFT FIELDER

★ ★

'There's nothing wrong with failing if you learn from it, and I've failed out here plenty.'

TRENT DILFER
GOLFER

'People are too hung up on winning. I can get off on a really good helmet throw.'

BILL LEE
MLB PITCHER

'I was reminded that when we lose and I strike out, a billion people in China don't care.'

REGGIE JACKSON
MLB RIGHT FIELDER

'Time heals all wounds, unless you pick at them.'

SHAUN ALEXANDER
NFL RUNNING BACK

★ ★

'I think someone should explain to the child that it's okay to make mistakes. That's how we learn. When we compete, we make mistakes.'

KAREEM ABDUL-JABBAR NBA CENTER

★ ★

'When I said my prayers as a kid, I'd tell the Lord I wanted to be a pro hockey player. Unfortunately, I forgot to mention National Hockey League, so I spent sixteen years in the minors.'

DON CHERRY NHL PLAYER, COACH AND COMMENTATOR

★ ★

'I can accept failure, everyone fails at something. But I can't accept not trying.'

MICHAEL JORDAN
NBA SHOOTING GUARD

'I think I fail a bit less than everyone else.'

JACK NICKLAUS
GOLFER

'Failure is good. It's fertilizer. Everything I've learned about coaching, I've learned from making mistakes.'

RICK PITINO
COLLEGE BASKETBALL COACH

'I had bad days on the field. But I didn't take them home with me. I left them in a bar along the way home.'

BOB LEMON
MLB PITCHER AND MANAGER

'The sun doesn't shine on the same dog's butt every day, but we sure didn't expect a total eclipse.'

STEVE SLOAN
COLLEGE FOOTBALL COACH

'I had slumps that lasted into the winter.'

BOB UECKER
MLB CATCHER AND BROADCASTER

'Failure happens all the time. It happens every day in practice. What makes you better is how you react to it.'

MIA HAMM
SOCCER FORWARD

'No one ever taught me and I can't teach anyone. If you can't explain it, how can you take credit for it?'

RED GRANGE
NFL HALFBACK

'I think an athlete should be honest. I know it's difficult, but if a guy knocked me on my can, I couldn't very well say I slipped.'

SUGAR RAY LEONARD WELTERWEIGHT BOXER

★ ★

'There's only one cure for what's wrong with all of us pitchers, and that's to take a year off. Then, after you've gone a year without throwing, quit altogether.'

JIM PALMER MLB PITCHER

★ ★

'Don't cut my throat, I may want to do that later myself.'

CASEY STENGEL
MLB OUTFIELDER AND MANAGER

'I'd like to say this was our worst game. Unfortunately, I can't.'

DON MATTINGLY
MLB FIRST BASEMAN AND COACH

'Never let your head hang down. Never give up and sit down and grieve. Find another way.'

SATCHEL PAIGE
MLB PITCHER

'Sometimes guys need to cry. Some hockey players think they're too tough to cry.'

BRETT HULL
NHL RIGHT WINGER

'My motto was always to keep swinging. Whether I was in a slump or feeling badly or having trouble off the field, the only thing to do was keep swinging.'

HANK AARON
MLB OUTFIELDER

'You're never a loser until you quit trying.'

MIKE DITKA
NFL PLAYER
AND COACH

'Nice guys finish last.'

LEO DUROCHER
MLB SHORTSTOP AND
MANAGER

'How would you like a job where, every time you make a mistake, a big red light goes on and 18,000 people boo?'

JACQUES PLANTE
NHL GOALIE

'I've missed more than 9,000 shots in my career. I've lost almost 300 games. Twenty-six times, I've been trusted to take the game winning shot and missed. I've failed over and over and over again in my life. And that is why I succeed.'

MICHAEL JORDAN NBA SHOOTING GUARD

FAME AND GLORY

'ALTHOUGH I WASN'T INVITED TO SHAKE HANDS WITH HITLER, I WASN'T INVITED TO THE WHITE HOUSE TO SHAKE HANDS WITH THE PRESIDENT EITHER.'

JESSE OWENS BLACK TRACK AND FIELD ATHLETE

'It's a weird scene. You win a few baseball games and all of a sudden you're surrounded by reporters and TV men with cameras asking you about Vietnam and race relations.'

VIDA BLUE
MLB PITCHER

'The 3,000 hitting thing was the first time I let individual pressure get to me. I was uptight about it. When I saw the hit going through, I had a sigh of relief more than anything.'

CARL YASTRZEMSKI
MLB LEFT FIELDER AND
FIRST BASEMAN

'I didn't really seek attention. I just wanted to play the game well and go home.'

KAREEM ABDUL-JABBAR
NBA CENTER

'On the field, blacks have been able to be super giants. But, once our playing days are over, this is the end of it and we go back to the back of the bus again.'

HANK AARON MLB OUTFIELDER

★ ★

'All I've done is run fast. I don't see why people should make much fuss about that.'

FANNY BLANKERS-KOEN
TRACK AND FIELD ATHLETE

'If you're successful in what you do over a period of time, you'll start approaching records, but that's not what you're playing for. You're playing to challenge and be challenged.'

LOU BROCK
MLB LEFT FIELDER

'I'm not interested in trying to work on people's perceptions. I am who I am, and if you don't take the time to learn about that, then your perception is going to be your problem.'

JIM BROWN
NFL RUNNING BACK AND
FULLBACK

'I'm hoping someday that some kid, black or white, will hit more home runs than myself. Whoever it is, I'd be pulling for him.'

HANK AARON
MLB OUTFIELDER

'The fame aspect of winning the Masters – besides being married and becoming a father, that's a strong third there.'

MIKE WEIR
GOLFER

'My career is an open book, but my life is not.'

BARRY BONDS
MLB LEFT FIELDER

'Shaking hands with the Queen of England was a long way from being forced to sit in the colored section of the bus going into downtown Wilmington, North Carolina.'

ALTHEA GIBSON
TENNIS PLAYER

★ ★

'I don't know where Hank Aaron will break Ruth's record but I can tell you one thing – ten years from the day he hits it three million people will say they were there.'

EDDIE MATHEWS MLB THIRD BASEMAN

★ ★

'I honestly didn't expect this much attention, but it just keeps happening so I must be doing something right.'

FREDDY ADU
SOCCER ATTACKING
MIDFIELDER AND STRIKER

"The real glory is being knocked to your knees and then coming back. That's real glory.'

VINCE LOMBARDI
NFL COACH AND GENERAL
MANAGER

'Fifty years from now I'll be just three inches of type in a record book.'

BROOKS ROBINSON
MLB THIRD BASEMAN

'When I lost my decathlon world record I took it like a man. I only cried for ten hours.'

DALEY THOMPSON
DECATHLETE

'If I feel strongly, I say it. I know I can do more good by being vocal than by staying quiet. I'd have a whole lot more money if I lied, but I wouldn't enjoy spending it.'

MARTINA NAVRATILOVA TENNIS PLAYER

★ ★

'I'm flattered that so many baseball people think I'm a Hall of Famer. But what's hard to believe is how 150-plus people have changed their minds about me since I became eligible, because I haven't had a base hit since then.'

RICHIE ASHBURN MLB OUTFIELDER

★ ★

'Honestly, at one time I though Babe Ruth was a cartoon character. I really did, I mean I wasn't born until 1961 and I grew up in Indiana.'

DON MATTINGLY
MLB FIRST BASEMAN
AND COACH

'I could ask the Phillies to keep me on to add to my statistics, but my love for the game won't let me do that.'

MIKE SCHMIDT
MLB THIRD BASEMAN

'I can remember a reporter asking me for a quote, and I didn't know what a quote was. I thought it was some kind of soft drink.'

JOE DIMAGGIO
MLB CENTER FIELDER

'I wish they'd shut the gates, and let us play ball with no press and no fans.'

RICHIE ALLEN
MLB FIRST AND THIRD BASEMAN

'Why do I have to be an example for your kid? You be an example for your own kid.'

BOB GIBSON
MLB PITCHER

'Kids should practice autographing baseballs. This is a skill that's often overlooked in Little League.'

TUG MCGRAW
MLB PITCHER

'I was a pretty good fighter. But it was the writers who made me great.'

JACK DEMPSEY
HEAVYWEIGHT BOXER

'This hand is not very active always, because it was in this hand that I carried my books. My carrying hand was always my strongest. Now I think my other hand has developed more muscles from signing all those autographs.'

HAILE GEBRSELASSIE RUNNER

★ ★

'I'm not a headline guy. I know that as long as I was following Ruth to the plate I could have stood on my head and no one would have known the difference.'

LOU GEHRIG MLB FIRST BASEMAN

★ ★

'I've seldom seen a horny player walk into a bar and not let out exactly what he did for a living.'

JOHNNY BENCH
MLB CATCHER

'I think I have already signed some scrap of paper for every man, woman, and child in the United States. What do they do with all those scraps of paper with my signature on it?'

VIDA BLUE
MLB PITCHER

'I don't care what you say about me. Just spell the name right.'

GENE SARAZEN
GOLFER

'I will tell you King's First Law of Recognition: You never get it when you want it, and then when it comes, you get too much.'

BILLIE JEAN KING
TENNIS PLAYER

FANS AND SUPPORTERS

'FANS DON'T BOO NOBODIES.' **REGGIE JACKSON** MLB PITCHER

'The eyes of some of the fans at Davis Cup matches scare me. There's no light in them. Fixed emotions. Blind worship. Horror. It makes me think of what happened to us long ago.'

BORIS BECKER
TENNIS PLAYER

'Always root for the winner. That way you won't be disappointed.'

TUG MCGRAW
MLB PITCHER

'You should enter a ballpark the way you enter a church.'

BILL LEE
MLB PITCHER

'The triple is the most exciting play in baseball. Home runs win a lot of games, but I never understood why fans are so obsessed with them.'

HANK AARON
MLB OUTFIELDER

'Baseball is like church. Many attend but few understand.'

WES WESTRUM
MLB MANAGER

'My Dad was my greatest supporter. He never put pressure on me.'

BOBBY ORR
NHL DEFENSEMAN

'There have been only two geniuses in the world: Willie Mays and Willie Shakespeare.'

TALLULAH BANKHEAD
ACTRESS

'We used to pray the White Sox and the Cubs would merge so Chicago would have only one bad team.'

TOM DREESEN
COMEDIAN

★ ★

'I love boxing. Where else do two grown men prance around in satin underwear, fighting over a belt? The one who wins gets a purse. They do it in gloves. It's the accessory connection I love.'

JOHN MCGOVERN COMEDIAN

★ ★

'If people don't want to come out to the ball park, nobody's gonna stop 'em.'

YOGI BERRA
MLB PLAYER AND MANAGER

'I firmly believe that respect is a lot more important, and a lot greater, than popularity.'

JULIUS ERVING
NBA SMALL FORWARD

'October is not only a beautiful month but marks the precious yet fleeting overlap of hockey, baseball, basketball, and football.'

JASON LOVE
HUMORIST

'If some- body in the crowd spits at you, you've got to swallow it.'

GARY LINEKER
SOCCER STRIKER AND BROADCASTER

'Kids are great. That's one of the best things about our business, all the kids you get to meet. It's a shame they have to grow up to be regular people and come to the games and call you names.'

CHARLES BARKLEY NBA FORWARD

★ ★

'A baseball fan has the digestive apparatus of a billy goat. He can, and does, devour any set of diamond statistics with insatiable appetite and then nuzzles hungrily for more.'

ARTHUR DALEY SPORTSWRITER

★ ★

'Boxing is like jazz. The better it is, the less people appreciate it.'

GEORGE FOREMAN
HEAVYWEIGHT BOXER

'Cubs fans are 90 percent scar tissue.'

GEORGE WILL
JOURNALIST AND COLUMNIST

'I owe everything I have to them when I'm out there on the mound. But I owe the fans nothing and they owe me nothing when I am not pitching.'

CHRISTY MATHEWSON
MLB PITCHER

'There is always some kid who may be seeing me for the first time. I owe him my best.'

JOE DIMAGGIO
MLB CENTER FIELDER

'As far as our fans are concerned, I'm the only one who counts; along with my teammates, obviously.'

ALESSANDRO DEL PIERO
SOCCER SECOND STRIKER

'Fans are the only ones who really care. There are no free-agent fans.'

DICK YOUNG
SPORTSWRITER

'One thing you learned as a Cubs fan: when you bought your ticket, you could bank on seeing the bottom of the ninth.'

JOE GARAGIOLA
MLB CATCHER AND BROADCASTER

'My parents are my backbone. Still are. They're the only group that will support you if you score zero or you score forty.'

KOBE BRYANT
NBA SHOOTING GUARD

★ ★

'Anyone can support a team that is winning – it takes no courage. But to stand behind a team, to defend a team when it is down and really needs you, that takes a lot of courage.'

BART STARR NFL QUARTERBACK AND COACH

★ ★

'Back then, my idol was Bugs Bunny, because I saw a cartoon of him playing ball – you know, the one where he plays every position himself with nobody else on the field but him? Now that I think of it, Bugs is still my idol. You have to love a ballplayer like that.'

NOMAR GARCIAPARRA MLB INFIELDER

★ ★

'The crowd makes the ballgame.'

TY COBB
MLB OUTFIELDER

'Don't send me flowers when I'm dead. If you like me, send them while I'm alive.'

BRIAN CLOUGH
SOCCER PLAYER AND MANAGER

'Say this for big league baseball – it is beyond any question the greatest conversation piece ever invented in America.'

BRUCE CATTON
HISTORIAN

'Nobody but you and your caddie cares what you do out there, and if your caddie is betting against you, he doesn't care, either.'

LEE TREVINO
GOLFER

LIFE AND DEATH

'COACHING IS NOT A NATURAL WAY OF LIFE. YOUR VICTORIES AND LOSSES ARE TOO CLEAR CUT.'

TOMMY PROTHRO NFL AND COLLEGE FOOTBALL COACH

'I asked my doctor how many more years I have left and he said, "You're too ornery to die."'

JIMMY PIERSALL
MLB OUTFIELDER

'When it comes to the game of life, I figure I've played the whole course.'

LEE TREVINO
GOLFER

'Our lives are not determined by what happens to us but how we react to what happens, not by what life brings us but the attitude we bring to life.'

WADE BOGGS
MLB THIRD BASEMAN

'The moment of victory is much too short to live for that and nothing else.'

PAAVO NURMI
RUNNER

'In life, so many things are taken for granted, but one thing I can honestly say is that I took every day, enjoyed the game of putting on that uniform and playing the great game of baseball.'

WADE BOGGS
MLB THIRD BASEMAN

'Life is not a spectator sport. If you're going to spend your whole life in the grandstand just watching what goes on, in my opinion you're wasting your life.'

JACKIE ROBINSON
MLB SECOND BASEMAN

'If I were to say, "God, why me?" about the bad things, then I should have said, "God, why me?" about the good things that happened in my life.'

ARTHUR ASHE
TENNIS PLAYER

'Hockey captures the essence of Canadian experience in the New World. In a land so inescapably and inhospitably cold, hockey is the chance of life, and an affirmation that despite the deathly chill of winter, we are alive.'

STEPHEN LEACOCK ECONOMIST AND HUMORIST

'If all I'm remembered for is being a good basketball player, then I've done a bad job with the rest of my life.'

ISIAH THOMAS
NBA POINT GUARD
AND COACH

'When a man wants to murder a tiger he calls it sport; when the tiger wants to murder him he calls it ferocity.'

GEORGE BERNARD SHAW
WRITER

'Life doesn't run away from nobody. Life runs at people.'

JOE FRAZIER
HEAVYWEIGHT BOXER

'You can't worry if it's cold; you can't worry if it's hot; you only worry if you get sick. Because then if you don't get well, you die.'

JOAQUIN ANDUJAR
MLB PITCHER

'My life had no meaning at all. I found only brief interludes of satisfaction. It was like my whole life had been about my whole basketball career.'

PETE MARAVICH NBA GUARD

★ ★

'Life is a gamble. You can get hurt, but people die in plane crashes, lose their arms and legs in car accidents; people die every day. Same with fighters: some die, some get hurt, some go on. You just don't let yourself believe it will happen to you.'

MUHAMMAD ALI HEAVYWEIGHT BOXER

★ ★

'People try to make a Greek tragedy of my life, and they can't do it. I'm too happy.'

CURT FLOOD
MLB CENTER FIELDER

'Being the first to cross the finish line makes you a winner in only one phase of life. It's what you do after you cross the line that really counts.'

RALPH BOSTON
TRACK AND FIELD ATHLETE

'Life doesn't give you all the practice races you need.'

JESSE OWENS
TRACK AND FIELD ATHLETE

'If you are first, you are first. If you are second, you are nothing.'

BILL SHANKLY
SOCCER MANAGER

103

'You spend a good piece of your life gripping a baseball and in the end it turns out that it was the other way around all the time.'

JIM BOUTON
MLB PITCHER

'Losing the Super Bowl is worse than death. With death, you don't have to get up next morning.'

GEORGE E. ALLEN
COLLEGE FOOTBALL COACH

'From what we get, we can make a living; what we give, however, makes a life.'

ARTHUR ASHE
TENNIS PLAYER

'A lot of my buddies also played golf, but when it came to going to the beach and chasing girls, they usually went that way and I went to the golf course.'

MIKE WEIR
GOLFER

'You know, a lot of people say they didn't want to die until the Red Sox won the World Series. Well, there could be a lot of busy ambulances tomorrow.'

JOHNNY DAMON MLB OUTFIELDER

★ ★

'If you are caught on a golf course during a storm and are afraid of lightning, hold up a 1-iron. Not even God can hit a 1-iron.'

LEE TREVINO GOLFER

★ ★

'Ain't no man can avoid being born average, but there ain't no man got to be common.'

SATCHEL PAIGE
MLB PITCHER

'The quality of a person's life is in direct proportion to their commitment to excellence, regardless of their chosen field of endeavor.'

VINCE LOMBARDI
NFL COACH AND
GENERAL MANAGER

'Baseball was 100 percent of my life.'

TY COBB
MLB OUTFIELDER

'If you step on people in this life, you're going to come back as a cockroach.'

WILLIE DAVIS
NFL DEFENSIVE END

'You learn about equality in history and civics, but you find out life is not really like that.'

ARTHUR ASHE
TENNIS PLAYER

'A life is not important except in the impact it has on other lives.'

JACKIE ROBINSON
MLB SECOND BASEMAN

'It is not the honor that you take with you, but the heritage you leave behind.'

BRANCH RICKEY
MLB CATCHER AND MANAGER

'At one point in your life, you'll have the thing you want or the reasons why you don't.'

ANDY RODDICK
TENNIS PLAYER

'The most rewarding things you do in life are often the ones that look like they cannot be done.'

ARNOLD PALMER GOLFER

LOSERS AND LOSING

'WHOEVER SAID, "IT'S NOT WHETHER YOU WIN OR LOSE THAT COUNTS," PROBABLY LOST.' **MARTINA NAVRATILOVA** TENNIS PLAYER

'When you're a winner you're always happy, but if you're happy as a loser you'll always be a loser.'

MARK FIDRYCH
MLB PITCHER

'Show me a good loser and I'll show you an idiot.'

LEO DUROCHER
MLB SHORTSTOP AND MANAGER

'What makes something special is not just what you have to gain, but what you feel there is to lose.'

ANDRE AGASSI
TENNIS PLAYER

'Finish last in your league and they call you Idiot. Finish last in medical school and they call you Doctor.'

ABE LEMONS
COLLEGE BASKETBALL COACH

'For myself, losing is not coming second. It's getting out of the water knowing you could have done better. For myself, I have won every race I've been in.'

IAN THORPE SWIMMER

★ ★

'Show me a good loser, and I'll show you a loser.'

VINCE LOMBARDI
NFL COACH

'No one knows what to say in the loser's locker room.'

MUHAMMAD ALI
HEAVYWEIGHT BOXER

'Most games are lost, not won.'

CASEY STENGEL
MLB PLAYER AND MANAGER

'I would not be bothered if we lost every game as long as we won the league.'

MARK VIDUKA
SOCCER FORWARD

'I don't mind getting beaten, but I hate to lose.'

REGGIE JACKSON
MLB PITCHER

'The joy of winning is not as dramatic as the losses were, because I expected us to win.'

JACK YOUNGBLOOD
NFL DEFENSIVE END

'You need to play with supreme confidence, or else you'll lose again, and then losing becomes a habit.'

JOE PATERNO
COLLEGE FOOTBALL COACH

'If you're afraid of losing, then you daren't win.'

BJORN BORG
TENNIS PLAYER

'If a tie is like kissing your sister, losing is like kissing your grandmother with her teeth out.'

GEORGE BRETT
MLB THIRD BASEMAN

★ ★

'Losing streaks are funny. If you lose at the beginning you got off to a bad start. If you lose in the middle of the season, you're in a slump. If you lose at the end, you're choking.'

GENE MAUCH MLB SECOND BASEMAN AND MANAGER

★ ★

'I never could stand losing. Second place didn't interest me. I had a fire in my belly.'

TY COBB
MLB OUTFIELDER

'I think everyone should experience defeat at least once during their career. You learn a lot from it.'

LOU HOLTZ
NFL AND COLLEGE
FOOTBALL COACH

'The Phillies beat the Cubs today in a doubleheader. That puts another keg in the Cubs' coffin.'

JERRY COLEMAN
MLB SECOND BASEMAN AND
BROADCASTER

'You're never as good as everyone tells you when you win, and you're never as bad as they say when you lose.'

LOU HOLTZ
NFL AND COLLEGE
FOOTBALL COACH

'I lost three times in my career. Losing to Holmes I could deal with, because I lost to a true champion.'

GERRY COONEY HEAVYWEIGHT BOXER

★ ★

'The fighter loses more than his pride in the fight; he loses part of his future. He's a step closer to the slum he came from.'

FLOYD PATTERSON LIGHT HEAVYWEIGHT AND HEAVYWEIGHT BOXER

★ ★

'Victory is fleeting. Losing is forever.'

BILLIE JEAN KING
TENNIS PLAYER

'Rockne wanted nothing but "bad losers." Good losers get into the habit of losing.'

GEORGE E. ALLEN
COLLEGE FOOTBALL COACH

'Without losers, where would the winners be?'

CASEY STENGEL
MLB OUTFIELDER AND MANAGER

'You can't win unless you learn how to lose.'

KAREEM ABDUL-JABBAR
NBA CENTER

'You can learn little from victory. You can learn everything from defeat.'

CHRISTY MATHEWSON
MLB PITCHER

'Been in this game one hundred years, but I see new ways to lose 'em I never knew existed before.'

CASEY STENGEL
MLB OUTFIELDER AND MANAGER

'You win some, lose some, and wreck some.'

DALE EARNHARDT
NASCAR DRIVER

'Winning is habit. Unfortunately, so is losing.'

VINCE LOMBARDI
NFL COACH

'Even Napoleon had his Watergate.'

YOGI BERRA
MLB PLAYER AND MANAGER

'The important thing is to learn a lesson every time you lose.'

JOHN McENROE
TENNIS PLAYER

'I never thought of losing, but now that it's happened, the only thing is to do it right. That's my obligation to all the people who believe in me. We all have to take defeats in life.'

MUHAMMAD ALI HEAVYWEIGHT BOXER

LOVE AND HAPPINESS

'I WISH PEOPLE WOULD LOVE EVERYBODY ELSE THE WAY THEY LOVE ME. IT WOULD BE A BETTER WORLD.'
MUHAMMAD ALI HEAVYWEIGHT BOXER

'A good professional athlete must have the love of a little boy. And the good players feel the kind of love for the game that they did when they were Little Leaguers.'

TOM SEAVER
MLB PITCHER

'Do you know what my favorite part of the game is? The opportunity to play.'

MIKE SINGLETARY
NFL PLAYER AND COACH

'My only day off is the day I pitch.'

ROGER CLEMENS
MLB PITCHER

'My wife doesn't care what I do when I'm away, as long as I don't have a good time.'

LEE TREVINO
GOLFER

113

'I once loved this game. But after being traded four times, I realized that it's nothing but a business. I treat my horses better than the owners treat us. It's a shame they've destroyed my love for the game.'

RICHIE ALLEN MLB FIRST AND THIRD BASEMAN

★ ★

'I always loved the game, but when my legs weren't hurting it was a lot easier to love.'

MICKEY MANTLE
MLB CENTER FIELDER AND FIRST BASEMAN

'What other people may find in poetry or art museums, I find in the flight of a good drive.'

ARNOLD PALMER
GOLFER

'After three failed marriages, I know what it's like to be replaced. So that's kind of how Joey Harrington must feel today.'

TERRY BRADSHAW
BROADCASTER AND NFL QUARTERBACK

'Either love your players or get out of coaching.'

BOBBY DODD
COLLEGE FOOTBALL COACH

'The first thing is to love your sport. Never do it to please someone else. It has to be yours.'

PEGGY FLEMING
FIGURE SKATER

'I just want to do what I do best, and that's fight. I love it.'

MIKE TYSON
HEAVYWEIGHT BOXER

'You don't suffer, kill yourself and take the risks I take just for money. I love bike racing.'

GREG LEMOND
CYCLIST

'Give me golf clubs, fresh air and a beautiful partner, and you can keep the clubs and the fresh air.'

JACK BENNY
COMEDIAN

★ ★

'Muhammad Ali was the kind of guy you either loved or hated, but you wanted to see him. I happen to really love him. He brought boxing to another level and always made you laugh.'

GERRY COONEY HEAVYWEIGHT BOXER

★ ★

'I love to hit people. I love to.'

MIKE TYSON
HEAVYWEIGHT BOXER

'Work? I never worked a day in my life. I always loved what I was doing, had a passion for it.'

ERBIE BANKS
SHORTSTOP AND FIRST BASEMAN

'Baseball, it is said, is only a game. True. And the Grand Canyon is only a hole in Arizona. Not all holes, or games, are created equal.'

GEORGE WILL
JOURNALIST AND COLUMNIST

'Girls had never been important. I'd had a girlfriend or two and had liked them a lot but it wasn't love, because my first love was tennis.'

BORIS BECKER
TENNIS PLAYER

'You always get a special kick on opening day, no matter how many you go through. You look forward to it like a birthday party when you're a kid. You think something wonderful is going to happen.'

JOE DIMAGGIO MLB CENTER FIELDER

★ ★

'The only football players in my time were fellows who really loved to play football. They were not in it for the money. There wasn't much money there. They would have played football for nothing.'

RED GRANGE NFL HALFBACK

★ ★

'Football is an incredible game. Sometimes it's so incredible, it's unbelievable.'

TOM LANDRY
NFL CORNERBACK AND COACH

'This is a game to be savored, not gulped. There's time to discuss everything between pitches or between innings.'

BILL VEECK
MLB CLUB OWNER

'I love the winning, I can take the losing, but most of all I love to play.'

BORIS BECKER
TENNIS PLAYER

'I get to play golf for a living. What more can you ask for – getting paid for doing what you love.'

TIGER WOODS
GOLFER

'People ask me what I do in winter when there's no baseball. I'll tell you what I do. I stare out the window and wait for spring.'

ROGERS HORNSBY
MLB SECOND BASEMAN AND MANAGER

'Finishing races is important, but racing is more important.'

DALE EARNHRDT
NASCAR DRIVER

'There are only two seasons – winter and baseball.'

BILL VEECK
MLB CLUB OWNER

'Too few of us realize what we have in golf, a game that provides small miracles of pleasure almost from the cradle to the grave.'

HUGH McILVANNEY
SCOTTISH SPORTSWRITER

'I was in the game for love. After all, where else can an old-timer with one leg, who can't hear or see, live like a king while doing the only thing I wanted to do?'

BILL VEECK MLB CLUB OWNER

★ ★

'Every player should be accorded the privilege of at least one season with the Chicago Cubs. That's baseball as it should be played – in God's own sunshine. And that's really living.'

ALVIN DARK MLB SHORTSTOP AND MANAGER

★ ★

'It is not the size of a man, but the size of his heart that matters.'

EVANDER HOLYFIELD
HEAVYWEIGHT BOXER

'I ain't ever had a job, I just always played baseball.'

SATCHEL PAIGE
MLB PITCHER

'The medals don't mean anything and the glory doesn't last. It's all about your happiness. My happiness is just loving the sport and having fun performing.'

JACKIE JOYNER KERSEE
ATHLETE

'I'm in trouble because I'm normal and slightly arrogant. A lot of people don't like themselves and I happen to be totally in love with myself.'

MIKE TYSON
HEAVYWEIGHT BOXER

119

MODESTY AND HUMILITY

'WHEN YOU'VE PLAYED THIS GAME FOR TEN YEARS AND GONE TO BAT SEVEN THOUSAND TIMES AND GOTTEN TWO THOUSAND HITS, DO YOU KNOW WHAT THAT REALLY MEANS? IT MEANS YOU'VE GONE ZERO FOR FIVE THOUSAND.'
REGGIE JACKSON MLB PITCHER

'First of all, I want to thank Tiger for not being here. That always makes things a little bit easier.'

SERGIO GARCIA
GOLFER

'The game embarrasses you until you feel inadequate.'

BEN CRENSHAW
GOLFER

'It is very dangerous to have your self-worth riding on your results as an athlete.'

JIM COURIER
TENNIS PLAYER

'No matter how great you are, the next great one is already sitting there waiting to take your place.'

JOE THEISMAN
NFL QUARTERBACK

'I was lucky enough to have the talent to play baseball. That's how I treated my career. I didn't think I was anybody special, anybody different.'

CARL YASTRZEMSKI
MLB LEFT FIELDER AND FIRST BASEMAN

'Most of my clichés aren't original.'

CHUCK KNOX
NFL COACH

'Babe Ruth was great. I'm just lucky.'

REGGIE JACKSON
MLB RIGHT FIELDER

'I'm just a four-wheel-drive pickup kind of guy, and so's my wife.'

MIKE GREENWELL
MLB OUTFIELDER

'I had pro offers from the Detroit Lions and Green Bay Packers, who were pretty hard up for linemen in those days. If I had gone into professional football the name Jerry Ford might have been a household word today.'

GERALD FORD PRESIDENT OF THE UNITED STATES

'Sometimes in this game it's as good to be lucky as it is to be good.'

VIDA BLUE
MLB PITCHER

'I owe a lot to my parents, especially my mother and father.'

GREG NORMAN
AUSTRALIAN GOLFER

'Don't measure yourself by what you have accomplished, but by what you should accomplish with your ability.'

JOHN WOODEN
COLLEGE BASKETBALL
COACH

'All we do is go out and play hard and play smart, and everyone thinks there's something special going on.'

DENNIS RODMAN
NBA SMALL FORWARD AND
POWER FORWARD

'After I hit a home run I had a habit of running the bases with my head down. I figured the pitcher already felt bad enough without me showing him up rounding the bases.'

MICKEY MANTLE MLB CENTER FIELDER AND FIRST BASEMAN

★ ★

'During my 18 years I came to bat almost 10,000 times. I struck out about 1,700 times and walked maybe 1,800 times. You figure a ballplayer will average about 500 at bats a season. That means I played seven years without ever hitting the ball.'

MICKEY MANTLE MLB OUTFIELDER AND FIRST BASEMAN

★ ★

'It's unbelievable how much you don't know about the game you've been playing all your life.'

MICKEY MANTLE
MLB CENTER FIELDER AND
FIRST BASEMAN

'To boast of a performance which I cannot beat is merely stupid vanity. And if I can beat it that means there is nothing special about it. What has passed is already finished with. What I find more interesting is what is still to come.'

EMIL ZATOPEK
RUNNER

'I feel greatly honored to have a ballpark named after me, especially since I've been thrown out of so many.'

CASEY STENGEL
MLB OUTFIELDER AND
MANAGER

'I'm often mentioned in the same sentence as Michael Jordan. You know, "That Scott Hastings, he's no Michael Jordan."'

SCOTT HASTINGS
NBA CENTER

'Somebody will always break your records. It is how you live that counts.'

EARL CAMPBELL
NFL RUNNING BACK

'I'm not an athlete. I'm a professional baseball player.'

JOHN KRUK
MLB FIRST BASEMAN AND OUTFIELDER

'It's a humbling thing being humble.'

MAURICE CLARETT
COLLEGE FOOTBALL PLAYER

'Home run hitters strike out a lot.'

REGGIE JACKSON
MLB PITCHER

★ ★

'I don't want to be Babe Ruth. He was a great ballplayer. I'm not trying to replace him. The record is there and damn right I want to break it, but that isn't replacing Babe Ruth.'

ROGER MARIS MLB OUTFIELDER

★ ★

'I think about the cosmic snowball theory. A few million years from now the sun will burn out and lose its gravitational pull. The earth will turn into a giant snowball and be hurled through space. When that happens it won't matter if I get this guy out.'

BILL LEE MLB PITCHER

★ ★

'Anybody with ability can play in the big leagues. But to be able to trick people year in and year out the way I did, I think that was a much greater feat.'

BOB UECKER
MLB CATCHER AND
BROADCASTER

'Professional golf is the only sport where, if you win 20 percent of the time, you're the best.'

JACK NICKLAUS
GOLFER

'It took me seventeen years to get three thousand hits in baseball. I did it in one afternoon on the golf course.'

HANK AARON
MLB OUTFIELDER

'I knew when my career was over. In 1965 my baseball card came out with no picture.'

BOB UECKER
MLB CATCHER AND BROADCASTER

'I went through life as a "player to be named later."'

JOE GARAGIOLA
MLB CATCHER

'I'm just like everybody else. I have two arms, two legs and 4,000 hits.'

PETE ROSE
MLB PLAYER AND MANAGER

'God was on our side more than them.'

ILYA KOVALCHUK
NHL LEFT WINGER

'Awards become corroded, friends gather no dust.'

JESSE OWENS
TRACK ATHLETE

'Sometimes I think if I had the same body and the same natural ability and someone else's brain, who knows how good a player I might have been.'

MICKEY MANTLE MLB CENTER FIELDER AND FIRST BASEMAN

MONEY AND WEALTH

'I'M TIRED OF HEARING ABOUT MONEY, MONEY, MONEY, MONEY. I JUST WANT TO PLAY THE GAME, DRINK PEPSI, WEAR REEBOK.' **SHAQUILLE O'NEAL** NBA CENTER

'You have to go broke three times to learn how to make a living.'

CASEY STENGEL
MLB OUTFIELDER AND MANAGER

'If I thought I had hurt my chances of winning another major just because I was chasing money around, I'd wind up kicking myself.'

MIKE WEIR
GOLFER

'I spent a lot of money on booze, birds and fast cars. The rest I just squandered.'

GEORGE BEST
SOCCER WINGER AND
ATTACKING MIDFIELDER

'What's unfortunate about buying a pitcher for $12 million is that he carries no warranty.'

BOB VERDI
SPORTSWRITER

'I can inspire people on how to use money, how to get economically powerful.'

MIKE TYSON
HEAVYWEIGHT BOXER

'How you play the game is for college ball. When you're playing for money, winning is the only thing that matters.'

LEO DUROCHER
MLB SHORTSTOP AND MANAGER

'I know a baseball star who wouldn't report the theft of his wife's credit cards because the thief spends less than she does.'

JOE GARAGIOLA
MLB CATCHER AND BROADCASTER

'You can have money piled to the ceiling, but the size of your funeral is still going to depend on the weather.'

CHUCK TANNER
MLB OUTFIELDER AND MANAGER

'If I weren't earning $3,000,000 a year to dunk a basketball, most people on the street would run in the other direction if they saw me coming.'

CHARLES BARKLEY NBA POWER FORWARD

★ ★

'If you do things with a certain type of result and cause a certain type of reaction or effect, then you increase your market value. It's very much a competition for the entertainment dollar, and that's never been more clearly evident than in today's NBA game.'

JULIUS ERVING NBA FORWARD

★ ★

'I'm the biggest fighter in the history of the sport. If you don't believe it, check the cash register.'

MIKE TYSON
HEAVYWEIGHT BOXER

'Sport must be amateur or it is not sport. Sports played professionally are entertainment.'

AVERY BRUNDAGE
TRACK AND FIELD ATHLETE

'Sporting goods companies pay me not to endorse their products.'

BOB UECKER
MLB CATCHER AND BROADCASTER

'I have a motto: Work to become, not to acquire.'

ALAN KULWICKI
NASCAR DRIVER

129

'When I was a kid in Houston, we were so poor we couldn't afford the last two letters, so we called ourselves po'.'

GEORGE FOREMAN HEAVYWEIGHT BOXER

★ ★

'The man who won't loan money isn't going to have many friends – or need them.'

WILT CHAMBERLAIN
NBA CENTER

'I call tennis the McDonald's of sport – you go in, they make a quick buck out of you, and you're out.'

PAT CASH
TENNIS PLAYER

'I'm going to win so much money this year, my caddie will make the top twenty money winner's list.'

LEE TREVINO
GOLFER

'My biggest win was getting the meal money bumped from $5 to $7.'

BOB COUSY
NBA POINT GUARD
AND COACH

'With the money I'm making, I should be playing two positions.'

PETE ROSE
MLB PLAYER AND MANAGER

'The only way to make money as a manager is to win in one place, get fired and hired somewhere else.'

WHITEY HERZOG
MLB OUTFIELDER AND MANAGER

'I regard golf as an expensive way of playing marbles.'

G.K. CHESTERTON
NOVELIST, POET AND JOURNALIST

'As soon as you take money for playing sport, it isn't sport, it's work.'

AVERY BRUNDAGE
TRACK AND FIELD ATHLETE

'I'm independently wealthy. I have enough money to last me the rest of my life – provided I die tomorrow.'

BILL FITCH NBA COACH

'For five years I've felt like the best prostitute in a high-class whorehouse. But all the other girls get paid more than I do.'

DENNIS RODMAN
NBA SMALL FORWARD AND
POWER FORWARD

'The three important elements of hockey are: forecheck, backcheck and paycheck.'

GILBERT PERRAULT
NHL CENTER

'The riskiest thing you can do is get greedy.'

LANCE ARMSTRONG
CYCLIST

'I could have played another year, but I would have been playing for the money, and baseball deserves better than that.'

GEORGE BRETT
MLB THIRD BASEMAN

'If money titles meant anything, I'd play more tournaments. The only thing that means a lot to me is winning. If I have more wins than anybody else and win more majors than anybody else in the same year, then it's been a good year.'

TIGER WOODS GOLFER

★ ★

'There is an old saying that money can't buy happiness. If it could, I would buy myself four hits every game.'

PETE ROSE MLB PLAYER AND MANAGER

★ ★

'Playing baseball for a living is like having a license to steal.'

PETE ROSE
MLB PLAYER AND MANAGER

'I'm the most loyal player money can buy.'

DON SUTTON
MLB PITCHER AND BROADCASTER

'Our expenses bill rose by 17 percent last year. How can it be right for top players to be earning £15m to £20m a year? It's crazy.'

MOHAMED AL-FAYED
SOCCER CHAIRMAN

'Always remember, money isn't everything – but also remember to make a lot of it before talking such fool nonsense.'

EARL WILSON
MLB PITCHER

MOTIVATION AND INSPIRATION

'A HUNGRY DOG HUNTS BEST.' **LEE TREVINO** GOLFER

'It's not my job to motivate players. They bring extraordinary motivation to our program. It's my job not to de-motivate them.'

LOU HOLTZ
NFL AND COLLEGE FOOTBALL COACH

'Motivation is simple. You eliminate those who are not motivated.'

LOU HOLTZ
NFL AND COLLEGE FOOTBALL COACH

'My inspiration was the game itself, not any individual player in it.'

NOMAR GARCIAPARRA
MLB INFIELDER

'A lot of people run a race to see who is fastest. I run to see who has the most guts, who can punish himself into exhausting pace, and then at the end, punish himself even more.'

STEVE PREFONTAINE
RUNNER

'*Experience tells you what to do; confidence allows you to do it.*'

STAN SMITH
TENNIS PLAYER

'*It is the best feeling in the world to have a close game come down to just a couple of plays and you are able to do it.*'

DREW BLEDSOE
NFL QUARTERBACK

'*I played basketball to try to get my parents from working so hard.*'

JAMES WORTHY
NBA SMALL FORWARD

'If you're paid before you walk on the court, what's the point in playing as if your life depended on it?'

ARTHUR ASHE
TENNIS PLAYER

'You can motivate by fear, and you can motivate by reward. But both those methods are only temporary. The only lasting thing is self-motivation.'

HOMER RICE NFL AND COLLEGE FOOTBALL COACH

'A person always doing his or her best becomes a natural leader, just by example.'

JOE DIMAGGIO
MLB CENTER FIELDER

'My responsibility is leadership, and the minute I get negative, that is going to have an influence on my team.'

DON SHULA
NFL CORNERBACK AND COACH

'You can't lead anyone else further than you have gone yourself.'

GENE MAUCH
MLB SECOND BASEMAN AND MANAGER

'I like my players to be married and in debt. That's the way you motivate them.'

ERNIE BANKS
MLB SHORTSTOP AND FIRST BASEMAN

'To be a leader, you have to make people want to follow you, and nobody wants to follow someone who doesn't know where he is going.'

JOE NAMATH NFL QUARTERBACK

★ ★

'I'll do whatever it takes to win games, whether it's sitting on a bench waving a towel, handing a cup of water to a teammate, or hitting the game-winning shot.'

KOBE BRYANT NBA SHOOTING GUARD

★ ★

'Leadership is getting someone to do what they don't want to do, to achieve what they want to achieve.'

TOM LANDRY
NFL CORNERBACK AND COACH

'Everybody kind of perceives me as being angry. It's not anger, it's motivation.'

ROGER CLEMENS
MLB PITCHER

'The difference between the impossible and the possible lies in a man's determination.'

TOMMY LASORDA
MLB PITCHER AND MANAGER

'Fear was absolutely necessary. Without it, I would have been scared to death.'

FLOYD PATTERSON
HEAVYWEIGHT BOXER

'A ball player's got to be kept hungry to become a big-leaguer. That's why no boy from a rich family ever made the big leagues.'

JOE DIMAGGIO
MLB CENTER FIELDER

'Being a professional is doing the things you love to do, on the days you don't feel like doing them.'

JULIUS ERVING
NBA SMALL FORWARD

'The ones who want to achieve and win championships motivate themselves.'

MIKE DITKA
NFL TIGHT END AND COACH

'The spirit, the will to win, and the will to excel are the things that endure. These qualities are so much more important than the events that occur.'

VINCE LOMBARDI
NFL COACH AND MANAGER

★ ★

'When someone tells me there is only one way to do things, it always lights a fire under my butt. My instant reaction is, I'm gonna prove you wrong.'

PICABO STREET SKIER

★ ★

'Money and women. They're two of the strongest things in the world. The things you do for a woman you wouldn't do for anything else. Same with money.'

SATCHEL PAIGE MLB PITCHER

★ ★

'I've always believed, no matter how many shots I miss, I'm going to make the next one.'

ISIAH THOMAS
NBA POINT GUARD AND COACH

'You can motivate players better with kind words than you can with a whip.'

BUD WILKINSON
NFL COACH

'I don't look at myself as a basketball coach. I look at myself as a leader who happens to coach basketball.'

MIKE KRZYZEWSKI
COLLEGE BASKETBALL COACH

'If I can't play for big money, I play for a little money. And if I can't play for a little money, I stay in bed that day.'

BOBBY RIGGS
TENNIS PLAYER

NOSTALGIA AND RETIREMENT

'I'LL PLAY OUT THE STRING AND LEAVE BASEBALL WITHOUT A TEAR. A MAN CAN'T PLAY GAMES HIS WHOLE LIFE.'
BROOKS ROBINSON MLB THIRD BASEMAN

'Boxing was not something I truly enjoyed. Like a lot of things in life, when you put the gloves on, it's better to give than to receive.'

SUGAR RAY LEONARD
WELTERWEIGHT BOXER

'All ballplayers should quit when it starts to feel as if all the baselines run uphill.'

BABE RUTH
MLB PITCHER AND OUTFIELDER

'The athlete of today is not an athlete alone. He's the center of a team – doctors, scientists, coaches, agents and so on.'

EMIL ZATOPEK
RUNNER

'I'm proud of what I achieved there, but a life built on memories is not much of a life.'

ERIC CANTONA
SOCCER FORWARD

'After 13 years, I couldn't accept to be Number Two.'

GUY LAFLEUR
NHL RIGHT WINGER

'I never want to quit playing ball. They'll have to cut this uniform off of me to get me out of it.'

ROY CAMPANELLA
MLB CATCHER

'All I can say to the young players is, enjoy every moment of it. Just enjoy every moment of it. Your career goes by very quickly.'

MARIO LEMIEUX
NHL CENTER

'Retire to what? I already play golf and fish for a living.'

JULIUS BOROS
GOLFER

'I don't even think about a retirement program because I'm working for the Lord, for the Almighty. And even though the Lord's pay isn't very high, his retirement program is, you might say, out of this world.'

GEORGE FOREMAN HEAVYWEIGHT BOXER

'The day I retire is the day I'll feel old. I'm not there yet.'

DOUG FLUTIE
NFL AND CFL QUARTERBACK

'When a man retires, his wife gets twice the husband but only half the income.'

CHI CHI RODRIGUEZ
GOLFER

'Baseball hasn't forgotten me. I go to a lot of old-timers games and I haven't lost a thing. I sit in the bullpen and let people throw things at me. Just like old times.'

BOB UECKER
MLB CATCHER AND BROADCASTER

'Before deciding to retire, stay home for a week and watch the daytime TV shows.'

BILL COPELAND
CRICKET UMPIRE

'All of the sports have a safety net, but boxing is the only sport that has none. So when the fighter is through, he is through. While he was fighting his management was very excited for him, but now that he is done, that management team is moving on.'

GERRY COONEY HEAVYWEIGHT BOXER

★ ★

'The trouble for today's footballers is they have too many distractions. We used to get our old players coming to watch training with football magazines in their hands. Now, more often than not, they are checking the share prices.'

FRANZ BECKENBAUER SOCCER SWEEPER, COACH AND MANAGER

★ ★

'Victory is everything. You can spend the money but you can never spend the memories.'

KEN VENTURI
GOLFER AND BROADCASTER

'I shouldn't say I'm looking forward to leading a normal life, because I don't know what normal is.'

MARTINA NAVRATILOVA
TENNIS PLAYER

'Boxing is for men, and is about men and is men. A celebration of the lost religion of masculinity all the more trenchant for being lost.'

JOYCE CAROL OATES
NOVELIST AND ESSAYIST

'If Casey Stengel were alive today, he'd be spinning in his grave.'

RALPH KINER
MLB OUTFIELDER

'I want to keep fighting because it is the only thing that keeps me out of the hamburger joints. If I don't fight, I'll eat this planet.'

GEORGE FOREMAN
HEAVYWEIGHT BOXER

'A nickel ain't worth a dime anymore.'

YOGI BERRA
MLB PLAYER AND MANAGER

'We signed to play until the day we died, and we did.'

JIMMY GREAVES
SOCCER STRIKER

'You can only milk a cow so long, then you're left holding the pail.'

HANK AARON
MLB OUTFIELDER

'I figure the faster I pedal, the faster I can retire.'

LANCE ARMSTRONG
CYCLIST

'Looking back on those days and little leaguer, the Hall of Fame is not even a blinking star, but through baseball travels and moving up the ladder, that star begins to flicker.'

WADE BOGGS MLB THIRD BASEMAN

★ ★

'I think one of the most difficult things for anyone who's played baseball is to accept the fact that maybe the players today are playing just as well as ever.'

RALPH KINER MLB OUTFIELDER

★ ★

'The way I figured it, I was even with baseball and baseball with me. The game had done much for me, and I had done much for it.'

JACKIE ROBINSON
MLB SECOND BASEMAN

'Baseball is drama with an endless run and an ever-changing cast.'

JOE GARAGIOLA
MLB CATCHER

'You always say, "I'll quit when I start to slide," and then one morning you wake up and realize you've done slid.'

SUGAR RAY ROBINSON
BOXER

'When I got to professional ball I used to play 150 games every year. It depends on how many games there was.'

WILLIE MAYS
MLB CENTER FIELDER

OPPONENTS AND ENEMIES

'TO BE THE BEST, YOU MUST FACE THE BEST. AND TO OVERCOME YOUR FEAR, YOU MUST DEAL WITH THE BEST.'
BARRY BONDS MLB LEFT FIELDER

'When you actually go in the ring, it's a very lonely and scary place. It's just you and the other guy.'

FRANK BRUNO
HEAVYWEIGHT BOXER

'When you've got your man down, rub him out.'

ROD LAVER
TENNIS PLAYER

'You are never really playing an opponent. You are playing yourself, your own highest standards, and when you reach your limits, that is real joy.'

ARTHUR ASHE
TENNIS PLAYER

'You don't play against opponents, you play against the game of basketball.'

BOBBY KNIGHT
COLLEGE BASKETBALL COACH

'Every great batter works on the theory that the pitcher is more afraid of him than he is of the pitcher.'

TY COBB
MLB OUTFIELDER

'Tall men come down to my height when I hit 'em in the body.'

JACK DEMPSEY
HEAVYWEIGHT BOXER

'I became a good pitcher when I stopped trying to make them miss the ball and started trying to make them hit it.'

SANDY KOUFAX
MLB PITCHER

'Sympathy is something that shouldn't be bestowed upon the Yankees. Apparently it angers them.'

BOB FELLER
MLB PITCHER

'You have no control over what the other guy does. You only have control over what you do.'

A. J. KITT ALPINE SKIER

'Guessing what the pitcher is going to throw is eighty percent of being a successful hitter. The other twenty percent is just execution.'

HANK AARON
MLB OUTFIELDER

'The pitcher has to find out if the hitter is timid, and if he is timid, he has to remind the hitter he's timid.'

DON DRYSDALE
MLB PITCHER

'It's always good to go against your friends, especially when you come out victorious.'

MICHAEL FINLEY
NBA GUARD AND FORWARD

'When you fear a foe, fear crushes your strength; and this weakness gives strength to your opponents.'

WILLIAM SHAKESPEARE
PLAYWRIGHT

'Buy a steak for a player on another club after the game, but don't even speak to him on the field. Get out there and beat them to death.'

LEO DUROCHER MLB SHORTSTOP AND MANAGER

★ ★

'You would be amazed how many important outs you can get by working the count down to where the hitter is sure you're going to throw to his weakness, and then throw to his power instead.'

WHITEY FORD MLB PITCHER

★ ★

'When I look at the net I don't see a goalie.'

PAVEL BURE
NHL RIGHT WINGER

'I never rooted against an opponent, but I never rooted for him either.'

ARNOLD PALMER
GOLFER

'When I came up to bat with three men on and two outs in the ninth, I looked in the other team's dugout and they were already in street clothes.'

BOB UECKER
MLB CATCHER AND
BROADCASTER

'I don't try to intimidate anybody before a fight. That's nonsense. I intimidate people by hitting them.'

MIKE TYSON
HEAVYWEIGHT BOXER

'I define fear as standing across the ring from Joe Louis and knowing he wants to go home early.'

MAX BAER
HEAVYWEIGHT BOXER

'You don't face Nolan Ryan without your rest. He's the only guy I go against that makes me go to bed before midnight.'

REGGIE JACKSON
MLB RIGHT FIELDER

'Show me a guy who's afraid to look bad, and I'll show you a guy you can beat every time.'

LOU BROCK
MLB LEFT FIELDER

'Anytime you've played in a place and you get a win against your old team, it feels good.'

CURTIS JOSEPH
NHL GOALIE

'I'm mad at Hank Aaron for deciding to play one more season. I threw him his last home run and thought I'd be remembered forever. Now, I'll have to throw him another.'

BILL LEE MLB PITCHER

★ ★

'Eighteen holes of match play will teach you more about your foe than 18 years of dealing with him across a desk.'

GRANTLAND RICE SPORTSWRITER

★ ★

'When I look at the net I see two or three goalies.'

RADEK DVORAK
NHL RIGHT WINGER

'Friendships are forgotten when the game begins.'

ALVIN DARK
MLB SHORTSTOP AND
MANAGER

'Son, what kind of pitch would you like to miss?'

DIZZY DEAN
MLB PITCHER

'It is how you show up at the showdown that counts.'

HOMER NORTON
COLLEGE FOOTBALL COACH

'Somebody's gotta win and somebody's gotta lose and I believe in letting the other guy lose.'

PETER ROSE
MLB PLAYER AND
MANAGER

RULES AND REFEREES

'BASEBALL IS ALMOST THE ONLY ORDERLY THING IN A VERY UNORDERLY WORLD. IF YOU GET THREE STRIKES, EVEN THE BEST LAWYER IN THE WORLD CAN'T GET YOU OFF.'
BILL VEECK MLB TEAM OWNER

'The fewer rules a coach has, the fewer rules there are for him to break.'

JOHN MADDEN
NFL PLAYER AND COACH

'I believe in rules. Sure I do. If there weren't any rules, how could you break them?'

LEO DUROCHER
MLB SHORTSTOP AND MANAGER

'Sure the fight was fixed. I fixed it with a right hand.'

GEORGE FOREMAN
HEAVYWEIGHT BOXER

'I never threw the spitter, well maybe once or twice when I really needed to get a guy out real bad.'

WHITEY FORD
MLB PITCHER

'Golf is like solitaire. When you cheat, you only cheat yourself.'

TONY LEMA
GOLFER

'I don't know if he throws a spitball, but he sure spits on the ball.'

CASEY STENGEL
MLB OUTFIELDER AND MANAGER

'You try to stay within the rules for the sake of the game, but you can always turn up the intensity.'

LAWRENCE TAYLOR
NFL OUTSIDE LINEBACKER

'In athletics there's always been a willingness to cheat if it looks like you're not cheating. I think that's just a quirk of human nature.'

KAREEM ABDUL-JABBAR
NBA CENTER

★ ★

'You can't sit on a lead and run a few plays into the line and just kill the clock. You've got to throw the ball over the goddamn plate and give the other man his chance. That's why baseball is the greatest game of them all.'

EARL WEAVER MLB MANAGER

★ ★

'If they play dirty, then you play dirty.'

LAWRENCE TAYLOR
NFL OUTSIDE LINEBACKER

'We're not attempting to circumcise the rules.'

BILL COWHER
NFL LINEBACKER AND COACH

'I never questioned the integrity of an umpire. Their eyesight, yes.'

LEO DUROCHER
MLB SHORTSTOP AND MANAGER

'It ain't nothin' 'til I call it.'

BILL KLEM
MLB UMPIRE

'The other day they asked me about mandatory drug testing. I said I believed in drug testing a long time ago. All through the sixties I tested everything.'

BILL LEE
MLB PITCHER

'Let's face it. Umpiring is not an easy or happy way to make a living. In the abuse they suffer, and the pay they get for it, you see an imbalance that can only be explained by their need to stay close to a game they can't resist.'

BOB UECKER MLB CATCHER AND BROADCASTER

★ ★

'Many baseball fans look upon an umpire as a sort of necessary evil to the luxury of baseball, like the odor that follows an automobile.'

CHRISTY MATHEWSON MLB PITCHER

★ ★

'In the olden days, the umpire didn't have to take any courses in mind reading. The pitcher told you he was going to throw at you.'

LEO DUROCHER
MLB SHORTSTOP AND
MANAGER

'Your job is to umpire for the ball and not the player.'

BILL KLEM
MLB UMPIRE

'We get criticized for showing no personality, then we get penalized when we do.'

LINDSAY DAVENPORT
TENNIS PLAYER

'I've cheated, or someone on my team has cheated, in almost every single game I've been in.'

ROGERS HORNSBY
MLB SECOND BASEMAN
AND MANAGER

155

'I made a game effort to argue, but two things were against me: the umpires and the rules.'

LEO DUROCHER
MLB SHORTSTOP AND MANAGER

'I never threw an illegal pitch. The trouble is, once in a while I toss one that ain't never been seen by this generation.'

SATCHEL PAIGE
MLB PITCHER

'We don't need refs, but I guess white guys need something to do.'

CHARLES BARKLEY
NBA FORWARD

'The best umpired game is the game in which the fans cannot recall the umpires who worked it.'

BILL KLEM
MLB UMPIRE

'No one respects the umpire's job more than I do; but, if I were a manager, I would probably be ejected three or four times a season fighting for my team.'

JIM EVANS MLB UMPIRE

★ ★

'I'd always have grease in at least two places, in case the umpires would ask me to wipe one off. I never wanted to be caught out there with anything though, it wouldn't be professional.'

GAYLORD PERRY MLB PITCHER

★ ★

'Steroids are for guys who want to cheat opponents.'

LAWRENCE TAYLOR
NFL OUTSIDE LINEBACKER

'The referee is going to be the most important person in the ring tonight besides the fighters.'

GEORGE FOREMAN
HEAVYWEIGHT BOXER

'The tradition of professional baseball always has been agreeably free of chivalry. The rule is, "Do anything you can get away with."'

HEYWOOD BROUN
NEW YORK SPORTSWRITER

'There are no opportune times for a penalty, and this is not one of those times.'

JACK YOUNGBLOOD
NFL DEFENSIVE END

SKILL AND TECHNIQUE

'I NEVER LOOKED AT THE CONSEQUENCES OF MISSING A BIG SHOT... WHEN YOU THINK ABOUT THE CONSEQUENCES YOU ALWAYS THINK OF A NEGATIVE RESULT.'

MICHAEL JORDAN NBA SHOOTING GUARD

'Speed is a great asset; but it's greater when it's combined with quickness – and there's a big difference.'

TY COBB
MLB OUTFIELDER

'Golf is not a game of good shots. It's a game of bad shots.'

BEN HOGAN
GOLFER

'Just take the ball and throw it where you want to. Throw strikes. Home plate don't move.'

SATCHEL PAIGE
MLB PITCHER

'The only way to maximize potential for performance is to be calm in the mind.'

BRIAN SIPE
NFL QUARTERBACK

'Nolan Ryan is pitching much better now that he has his curve ball straightened out.'

JOE GARAGIOLA
MLB CATCHER AND BROADCASTER

'It's only a hitch when you're in a slump. When you're hitting the ball it's called rhythm.'

EDDIE MATHEWS
MLB THIRD BASEMAN

'It took me a few years to realize that throwing harder wasn't always better.'

DENNIS ECKERSLEY
MLB PITCHER

'It helps if the hitter thinks you're a little crazy.'

NOLAN RYAN
MLB PITCHER

'There is no room in your mind for negative thoughts. The busier you keep yourself with the particulars of shot assessment and execution, the less chance your mind has to dwell on the emotional. This is sheer intensity.'

JACK NICKLAUS GOLFER

'The way to catch a knuckleball is to wait until it stops rolling and then pick it up.'

BOB UECKER
MLB CATCHER AND BROADCASTER

'I was not successful as a ballplayer, as it was a game of skill.'

CASEY STENGEL
MLB OUTFIELDER AND MANAGER

'It's my job to get us in good plays, or more importantly, out of bad plays.'

DREW BREES
NFL QUARTERBACK

'The best and fastest way to learn a sport is to watch and imitate a champion.'

JEAN-CLAUDE KILLY
SKIER

'In the beginning I used to make one terrible play a game. Then I got so I'd make one a week and finally I'd pull a bad one about once a month. Now, I'm trying to keep it down to one a season.'

LOU GEHRIG MLB FIRST BASEMAN

★ ★

'People talk about skating, puck handling and shooting, but the whole sport is angles and caroms, forgetting the straight direction the puck is going, calculating where it will be directed, factoring in all the interruptions. Basically, my whole game is angles.'

WAYNE GRETZKY NHL CENTER AND COACH

★ ★

'Hitting is timing. Pitching is upsetting timing.'

WARREN SPAHN
MLB PITCHER

'Anybody's best pitch is the one the batters ain't hitting that day.'

CHRISTY MATHEWSON
MLB PITCHER

'Tim Henman needs to shut out the voices he doesn't need to hear. I had the single-minded focus he's trying to find.'

PETE SAMPRAS
TENNIS PLAYER

'It's fool's gold if you are winning games and are not playing the right way.'

ANTONIO DAVIS
NBA POWER FORWARD AND CENTER

'You give 100 percent in the first half of the game, and if that isn't enough in the second half you give what's left.'

YOGI BERRA
MLB PLAYER AND COACH

'The strong take from the weak and the smart take from the strong.'

PETE CARRIL
NBA AND COLLEGE BASKETBALL COACH

'Some people skate to the puck. I skate to where the puck is going to be.'

WAYNE GRETZKY
NHL CENTER

'The idea is not to block every shot. The idea is to make your opponent believe that you might block every shot.'

BILL RUSSELL
NBA CENTER

'There are two theories on hitting the knuckleball. Unfortunately, neither of them works.'

CHARLEY LAU MLB CATCHER AND COACH

★ ★

'Hockey is an art. It requires speed, precision, and strength like other sports, but it also demands an extraordinary intelligence to develop a logical sequence of movements, a technique which is smooth, graceful and in rhythm with the rest of the game.'

JACQUES PLANTE NHL GOALIE

★ ★

'I know I am getting better at golf because I am hitting fewer spectators.'

GERALD FORD
PRESIDENT OF THE UNITED STATES

'Half the game is mental; the other half is being mental.'

JIM MCKENNY
NHL DEFENSEMAN

'If my uniform doesn't get dirty, I haven't done anything in the baseball game.'

RICKEY HENDERSON
MLB LEFT FIELDER AND COACH

'There's more to boxing than hitting. There's not getting hit, for instance.'

GEORGE FOREMAN
HEAVYWEIGHT BOXER

'The only difference between a good shot and a bad shot is if it goes in or not.'

CHARLES BARKLEY
NBA POWER FORWARD

'I had some friends here from North Carolina who'd never seen a homer, so I gave them a couple.'

CATFISH HUNTER
MLB PITCHER

'Ninety percent of the game is half mental.'

YOGI BERRA
MLB PLAYER AND MANAGER

'Sliding headfirst is the safest way to get to the next base, and the fastest. You don't lose your momentum, and there's one more important reason I slide headfirst, it gets my picture in the paper.'

PETE ROSE
MLB PLAYER AND MANAGER

★ ★

'Getting hit motivates me. It makes me punish the guy more. A fighter takes a punch, hits back with three punches.'

ROBERTO DURAN LIGHTWEIGHT BOXER

STRESS AND PRESSURE

'COACHING IN THE NBA IS NOT EASY. IT'S LIKE A NERVOUS BREAKDOWN WITH A PAYCHECK.'

PAT WILLIAMS NBA MANAGER

'As a part owner, I'm going to be not only an admirer, but a nervous wreck.'

ROGER STAUBACH
NFL QUARTERBACK AND
NASCAR TEAM OWNER

'If the coach is good, I don't think a psychologist is needed.'

HANSIE CRONJE
CRICKET PLAYER

'For the parent of a Little Leaguer, a baseball game is simply a nervous breakdown divided into innings.'

EARL WILSON
MLB PITCHER

'Pressure is playing for ten dollars when you don't have a dime in your pocket.'

LEE TREVINO
GOLFER

'If you can't stand the heat in the dressing room, get out of the kitchen.'

TERRY VENABLES
SOCCER PLAYER AND MANAGER

'I'm not really interested in sports psychology. It makes me feel like a crazy person.'

MICHELE WIE
GOLFER

'I will never have a heart attack. I give them.'

GEORGE STEINBRENNER
OWNER OF THE NEW YORK YANKEES

'Pressure is healthy. It can lead to improvement. Stress is unhealthy. It can lead to mistakes.'

JOHN WOODEN
COLLEGE BASKETBALL COACH

'You find that you have peace of mind and can enjoy yourself, get more sleep, rest when you know that it was a one hundred percent effort that you gave – win or lose.'

GORDIE HOWE NHL RIGHT WINGER

★ ★

'All of us get knocked down, but it's resiliency that really matters. All of us do well when things are going well, but the thing that distinguishes athletes is the ability to do well in times of great stress, urgency and pressure.'

ROGER STAUBACH NFL QUARTERBACK

★ ★

'Golf has probably kept more people sane than psychiatrists have.'

HARVEY PENICK
GOLFER

'A full mind is an empty bat.'

BRANCH RICKEY
MLB CATCHER AND MANAGER

'Luck? Sure. But only after long practice and only with the ability to think under pressure.'

BABE ZAHARIAS
TRACK AND FIELD ATHLETE

'Some people think they are concentrating when they're merely worrying.'

BOBBY JONES
GOLFER

'The great American game should be an unrelenting war of nerves.'

TY COBB
MLB OUTFIELDER

'I don't like money, actually, but it quiets my nerves.'

JOE LOUIS
HEAVYWEIGHT BOXER

'Therapy can be a good thing; it can be therapeutic.'

ALEX RODRIGUEZ
MLB THIRD BASEMAN

'Concentration is a fine antidote to anxiety.'

JACK NICKLAUS
GOLFER

'Why should a player be denied the sheer pleasure and release of smashing his own expensive racket into pieces occasionally?'

PETER USTINOV
ACTOR AND AUTHOR

★ ★

'To play well you must feel tranquil and at peace. I have never been troubled by nerves in golf because I felt I had nothing to lose and everything to gain.'

HARRY VARDON GOLFER

★ ★

'In baseball, my theory is to strive for consistency, not to worry about the numbers. If you dwell on statistics you get shortsighted, if you aim for consistency, the numbers will be there at the end.'

TOM SEAVER MLB PITCHER

★ ★

'There is a lot of pressure put on me, but I don't put a lot of pressure on myself. I feel if I play my game, it will take care of itself.'

LEBRON JAMES
NBA SMALL FORWARD

'Serenity is knowing that your worst shot is still pretty good.'

JOHNNY MILLER
GOLFER

'If your stomach disputes you, lie down and pacify it with cool thoughts.'

SATCHEL PAIGE
MLB PITCHER

'The ballplayer who loses his head, who can't keep his cool, is worse than no ballplayer at all.'

LOU GEHRIG
MLB FIRST BASEMAN

'Sometimes the biggest problem is in your head. You've got to believe you can play a shot instead of wondering where your next bad shot is coming from.'

JACK NICKLAUS
GOLFER

'Right out of high school I never had the fear of getting beat, which is how most people lose.'

DAN GABLE
WRESTLER

'It's supposed to be fun. The man says, "Play Ball" not "Work Ball" you know.'

WILLIE STARGELL
MLB LEFT FIELDER AND FIRST BASEMAN

'Before I pitch any game, from spring training to Game Seven of the World Series, I'm scared to death.'

CURT SCHILLING
MLB PITCHER

★ ★

'I always feel pressure. If you don't feel nervous, that means you don't care about how you play. I care about how I perform. I've always said the day I'm not nervous playing is the day I quit.'

TIGER WOODS GOLFER

SUCCESS AND THE SUCCESSFUL

'THERE ARE NO TRAFFIC JAMS ALONG THE EXTRA MILE.'
ROGER STAUBACH NFL QUARTERBACK

'The key to success is to keep growing in all areas of life – mental, emotional, spiritual, as well as physical.'

JULIUS ERVING
NBA SMALL FORWARD

'Don't mistake activity for achievement.'

JOHN WOODEN
COLLEGE BASKETBALL COACH

'It's not whether you get knocked down; it's whether you get back up.'

VINCE LOMBARDI
NFL COACH AND GENERAL MANAGER

'Some people want it to happen, some wish it would happen, others make it happen.'

MICHAEL JORDAN
NBA SHOOTING GUARD

'Everyone has a breaking point, turning point, stress point... the game is permeated with it. The fans don't see it because we make it look so efficient. But internally, for a guy to be successful, you have to be like a clock spring, wound but not loose at the same time.'

DAVE WINFIELD MLB OUTFIELDER

★ ★

'The difference between a successful person and others is not a lack of strength, not a lack of knowledge, but rather a lack of will.'

VINCE LOMBARDI
NFL COACH AND GENERAL MANAGER

'A lot of the things that until now seemed unthinkable are starting to be thinkable.'

NICK JOHNSON
MLB FIRST BASEMAN

'Normally, if you go through a game without attracting attention, you are doing a hell of a job.'

JERRY KRAMER
NFL GUARD AND KICKER

'I'm not afraid to be lonely at the top.'

BARRY BONDS
MLB LEFT FIELDER

'Everybody loves success,
but they hate successful
people.'

JOHN M^cENROE
TENIS PLAYER

'Success is not the result
of spontaneous
combustion. You must
first set yourself on fire.'

FRED SHERO
NHL DEFENSEMAN AND
COACH

'The secret of my success
was clean living and
a fast outfield.'

LEFTY GOMEZ
MLB PITCHER

'Nobody has milked one performance better than me – and I'm damned proud of it.'

BRUCE JENNER
TRACK AND FIELD
ATHLETE

★ ★

'Once you agree upon the price you and your family must pay for
success, it enables you to ignore the minor hurts, the
opponent's pressure, and the temporary failures.'

VINCE LOMBARDI NFL COACH AND GENERAL MANAGER

★ ★

'Perhaps the truest axiom in baseball is that the toughest thing to do is repeat.'

WALT ALSTON
MLB FIRST BASEMAN AND MANAGER

'Your bat is your life. It's your weapon. You don't want to go into battle with anything that feels less than perfect.'

LOU BROCK
MLB LEFT FIELDER

'Besides pride, loyalty, discipline, heart, and mind, confidence is the key to all the locks.'

JOE PATERNO
COLLEGE FOOTBALL COACH

'A successful coach needs a patient wife, loyal dog, and great quarterback – and not necessarily in that order.'

BUD GRANT
CFL AND NFL PLAYER AND COACH

'The dictionary is the only place that success comes before work. Hard work is the price we must pay for success. I think you can accomplish anything if you're willing to pay the price.'

VINCE LOMBARDI NFL COACH AND GENERAL MANAGER

★ ★

'I had to fight all my life to survive. They were all against me, but I beat the bastards and left them in the ditch.'

TY COBB MLB OUTFIELDER

★ ★

'The road to success runs uphill.'

WILLIE DAVIS
NFL DEFENSIVE END

'The greatest stimulator of my running career was fear.'

HERB ELLIOTT
RUNNER

'Success isn't something that just happens – success is learned, success is practiced and then it is shared.'

SPARKY ANDERSON
MLB SECOND BASE-MAN AND MANAGER

'Toughness is in the soul and spirit, not in muscles.'

ALEX KARRAS
NFL DEFENSIVE TACKLE

'It is nothing new or original to say that golf is played one stroke at a time. But it took me many years to realize it.'

BOBBY JONES
GOLFER

'The harder you work, the harder it is to surrender.'

VINCE LOMBARDI
NFL COACH AND GENERAL MANAGER

'The man who has no imagination has no wings.'

MUHAMMAD ALI
HEAVYWEIGHT BOXER

'Success is about having, excellence is about being. Success is about having money and fame, but excellence is being the best you can be.'

MIKE DITKA
NFL COACH

'Great champions have an enormous sense of pride. The people who excel are those who are driven to show the world and prove to themselves just how good they are.'

NANCY LOPEZ GOLFER

★ ★

'The price of success is hard work, dedication to the job at hand, and the determination that whether we win or lose, we have applied the best of ourselves to the task at hand.'

VINCE LOMBARDI NFL COACH AND GENERAL MANAGER

★ ★

'The most important key to achieving great success is to decide upon your goal and launch, get started, take action, move.'

JOHN WOODEN
COLLEGE BASKETBALL COACH

'The formula for success is simple: practice and concentration then more practice and more concentration.'

BABE ZAHARIAS
TRACK AND FIELD ATHLETE

'Success is a journey, not a destination. The doing is often more important than the outcome.'

ARTHUR ASHE
TENNIS PLAYER

TEAMWORK AND TEAMMATES

'FINDING GOOD PLAYERS IS EASY. GETTING THEM TO PLAY AS A TEAM IS ANOTHER STORY.'

CASEY STENGEL MLB OUTFIELDER AND MANAGER

'Chemistry is a class you take in high school or college, where you figure out two plus two is ten, or something.'

DENNIS RODMAN
NBA SMALL FORWARD AND
POWER FORWARD

'A coach's main job is to reawaken a spirit in which the players can blend together effortlessly.'

PHIL JACKSON
NBA FORWARD AND COACH

'Any time Detroit scores more than 100 points and holds the other team below 100 points they almost always win.'

DOUG COLLINS
NBA PLAYER AND COACH

'It's all about chemistry. Talent alone won't get it done.'

BRETT FAVRE
NFL QUARTERBACK

'One man can be a crucial ingredient on a team, but one man cannot make a team.'

KAREEM ABDUL-JABBAR
NBA CENTER

'Commitment to the team – there is no such thing as in-between, you are either in or out.'

PAT RILEY
NBA PLAYER AND COACH

'There's a great deal of love for one another on this club. Perhaps we're living in Camelot.'

JERRY KRAMER
NFL GUARD AND KICKER

'A team is where a boy can prove his courage on his own. A gang is where a coward goes to hide.'

MICKEY MANTLE
MLB CENTER FIELDER AND FIRST BASEMAN

★ ★

'It's hard to get people to overcome the thought that they have to take care of themselves first. It's hard to get players to give in to the group and become selfless as opposed to selfish.'

ISIAH THOMAS NBA POINT GUARD AND COACH

★ ★

'Team guts always beat individual greatness.'

BOB ZUPPKE
COLLEGE FOOTBALL COACH

'Good teams become great ones when the members trust each other enough to surrender the "me" for the "we."'

PHIL JACKSON
NBA FORWARD AND COACH

'Basketball is a team game. But that doesn't mean all five players should have the same amount of shots.'

DEAN SMITH
COLLEGE BASKETBALL COACH

'You watch some teams these days and you wonder if they just met on the playground and decided to choose up sides.'

DENNIS RODMAN
NBA SMALL FORWARD AND POWER FORWARD

'To all the positions, I just bring the determination to win. Me being an unselfish player, I think that can carry on to my teammates. When you have one of the best players on the court being unselfish, I think that transfers to the other players.'

LEBRON JAMES NBA SMALL FORWARD

★ ★

'Great players are willing to give up their own
personal achievement for the achievement of the group.
It enhances everybody.'

KAREEM ABDUL-JABBAR NBA CENTER

★ ★

*'Sometimes a player's
greatest challenge is coming
to grips with his role on
the team.'*

SCOTTIE PIPPEN
NBA FORWARD

*'Only in baseball can a team
player be a pure individualist
first and a team player
second, within the rules
and spirit of the game.'*

BRANCH RICKEY
MLB CATCHER AND MANAGER

*'Individual glory is insignificant
when compared to achieving
victory as a team.'*

DOT RICHARDSON
SOFTBALL PLAYER

*'I'm just a
ballplayer
with one
ambition, and
that is to give
all I've got to
help my ball
club win.
I've never
played any
other way.'*

JOE DIMAGGIO
MLB CENTER FIELDER

'You can't win if nobody catches the ball in the outfield. You're only as good as the team you have behind you.'

JIM PALMER
MLB PITCHER

'The winning team has a dedication. It will have a core of veteran players who set the standards. They will not accept defeat.'

MERLIN OLSEN
NFL DEFENSIVE TACKLE

'The achievements of an organization are the results of the combined effort of each individual.'

VINCE LOMBARDI
NFL COACH AND GENERAL MANAGER

'Individual commitment to a group effort – that is what makes a team work.'

VINCE LOMBARDI
NFL COACH AND GENERAL MANAGER

'There's nothing greater in the world than when somebody on the team does something good, and everybody gathers around to pat him on the back.'

BILLY MARTIN MLB SECOND BASEMAN AND MANAGER

★ ★

'Last year we had so many people coming in and out they didn't bother to sew their names on the backs of the uniforms. They just put them there with Velcro.'

ANDY VAN SLYKE MLB OUTFIELDER AND COACH

★ ★

'Ask not what your teammates can do for you. Ask what you can do for your teammates.'

MAGIC JOHNSON
NBA POINT GUARD

'The secret of winning football games is working more as a team, less as individuals. I play not my eleven best, but my best eleven.'

KNUTE ROCKNE
COLLEGE FOOTBALL COACH

'The strength of the group is the strength of the leaders.'

VINCE LOMBARDI
NFL COACH AND GENERAL MANAGER

'A team will always appreciate a great individual if he's willing to sacrifice for the group.'

KAREEM ABDUL-JABBAR
NBA CENTER

183

'As brilliant an individual that Michael Jordan was, he was not successful until he got with a good team unit.'

KAREEM ABDUL-JABBAR
NBA CENTER

'It's about the team. I can give the leadership and the direction, but the team has to gel. That means keeping them together, able to live with each other in the same room, get the best from each other.'

SIR ALEX FERGUSON
SOCCER COACH

'The way a team plays as a whole determines its success. You may have the greatest bunch of individual stars in the world, but if they don't play together, the club won't be worth a dime.'

BABE RUTH
MLB PITCHER

'There's been a lot of talk of me being a one-man show but that's simply not the case. We win games when I score 40 points and we've won when I score ten.'

KOBE BRYANT NBA SHOOTING GUARD

TRAINING AND PRACTICE

'MOST PEOPLE HAVE THE WILL TO WIN, FEW HAVE THE WILL TO PREPARE TO WIN.' **BOBBY KNIGHT** COLLEGE BASKETBALL COACH

'You can't make a great play unless you do it first in practice.'

CHUCK NOLL
NFL PLAYER AND COACH

'I hated every minute of training, but I said, "Don't quit. Suffer now and live the rest of your life as a champion."'

MUHAMMAD ALI
HEAVYWEIGHT BOXER

'A month before the season I stop putting ketchup on my french fries.'

MARIO LEMIEUX
NHL CENTER

'The way to make coaches think you're in shape in the spring is to get a tan.'

WHITEY FORD
MLB PITCHER

'I know my players don't like my practices, but that's okay because I don't like their games'

HARRY NEALE
NHL COACH AND BROADCASTER

'I don't generally like running. I believe in training by rising gently up and down from the bench.'

SATCHEL PAIGE
MLB PITCHER

'The time when there is no one there to feel sorry for you or to cheer for you is when a player is made.'

TIM DUNCAN
NBA FORWARD

'In theory there is no difference between theory and practice. In practice there is.'

YOGI BERRA
MLB PLAYER AND MANAGER

'I played everything. I played lacrosse, baseball, hockey, soccer, track and field. I was a big believer that you played hockey in the winter and when the season was over you hung up your skates and you played something else.'

WAYNE GRETZKY NHL CENTER AND COACH

★ ★

'They say, "Practice makes perfect." Of course, it doesn't. For the vast majority of golfers it merely consolidates imperfection.'

HENRY LONGHURST POLITICIAN AND SPORTSWRITER

★ ★

'Spectacular achievements are always preceded by unspectacular preparation.'

ROGER STAUBACH
NFL QUARTERBACK

'Some guys practice like all-Americans but they can't play.'

JOE MONTANA
NFL QUARTERBACK

'I'm gaining weight the right way: I'm drinking beer.'

JOHNNY DAMON
MLB OUTFIELDER

'Some people like going to the pub; I enjoy going to the gym.'

FRANK BRUNO
HEAVYWEIGHT BOXER

'Gold medals are awarded in the summer, but they're earned in the winter.'

KYLE HAMILTON
ROWER

'*What a player does best, he should practice least. Practice is for problems.*'

DUKE SNIDER
MLB OUTFIELDER

'*When I'm not in training, I'll walk around the streets at 153, but it's not solid; it's my socializing weight.*'

SUGAR RAY LEONARD
WELTERWEIGHT BOXER

'*One day of practice is like one day of clean living. It doesn't do you any good.*'

ABE LEMMONS
COLLEGE BASKETBALL COACH

'*It's not necessarily the amount of time you spend at practice that counts; it's what you put into the practice.*'

ERIC LINDROS
NHL CENTER

★ ★

'The fight is won or lost far away from witnesses – behind the lines, in the gym, and out there on the road, long before I dance under those lights.'

MUHAMMAD ALI HEAVYWEIGHT BOXER

★ ★

'If you could equate the amount of time and effort put in mentally and physically into succeeding on the baseball field and measured it by the dirt on your uniform, mine would have been black.'

MIKE SCHMIDT MLB THIRD BASEMAN

★ ★

'Discipline yourself and others won't need to.'

JOHN WOODEN
COLLEGE BASKETBALL COACH

'The most prepared are the most dedicated.'

RAYMOND BERRY
NFL WIDE RECEIVER

'If you train hard, you'll not only be hard, you'll be hard to beat.'

HERSCHEL WALKER
NFL RUNNING BACK

'I'm exhausted trying to stay healthy.'

STEVE YZERMAN
NHL CENTER

'They say that nobody is perfect. Then they tell you practice makes perfect. I wish they'd make up their minds.'

WILT CHAMBERLAIN
NBA CENTER

'I'm not out there sweating for three hours every day just to find out what it feels like to sweat.'

MICHAEL JORDAN
NBA SHOOTING GUARD

'For every pass I caught in a game, I caught a thousand in practice.'

DON HUTSON
NFL WIDE RECEIVER, SAFETY, AND PLACEKICKER

'Correct one fault at a time. Concentrate on the one fault you want to overcome.'

SAM SNEAD
GOLFER

'If you're not practicing, somebody else is, somewhere, and he'll be ready to take your job.'

BROOKS ROBINSON
MLB THIRD BASEMAN

'To give yourself the best possible chance of playing to your potential, you must prepare for every eventuality. That means practice.'

SEVE BALLESTEROS GOLFER

VIOLENCE AND PAIN

'THE MAN WHO CAN DRIVE HIMSELF FURTHER ONCE THE EFFORT GETS PAINFUL IS THE MAN WHO WILL WIN.
ROGER BANNISTER SPRINTER

'If hockey fights were fake, you would see me in more of them.'

ROD GILBERT
NHL RIGHT WINGER

'Skiing combines outdoor fun with knocking down trees with your face.'

DAVE BARRY
HUMORIST

'The only way you can check Gretzky is to hit him when he is standing still singing the national anthem.'

HARRY SINDEN
NHL COACH AND GENERAL MANAGER

'We get nose jobs all the time in the NHL, and we don't even have to go to the hospital.'

BRAD PARK
NHL DEFENSEMAN

'If they knocked two of your guys down, I'd get four. You have to protect your hitters.'

DON DRYSDALE
MLB PITCHER

'Somebody hits me, I'm going to hit him back. Even if it does look like he hasn't eaten in a while.'

CHARLES BARKLEY
NBA POWER FORWARD

'Boxing is the only sport you can get your brain shook, your money took and your name in the undertaker book.'

JOE FRAZIER
HEAVYWEIGHT BOXER

'Sure there have been injuries and deaths in boxing – but none of them serious.'

ALAN MINTER
MIDDLEWEIGHT BOXER

'Baseball is a game, yes. It is also a business. But what it most truly is is disguised combat. For all its gentility, its almost leisurely pace, baseball is violence under wraps.'

WILLIE MAYS MLB CENTER FIELDER

★ ★

'Taking them out of the picture, so to speak, what football really is, the savagery, the core root of football, it doesn't change. It really puts the real in football.'

LAWRENCE TAYLOR NFL OUTSIDE LINEBACKER

★ ★

'When you win, nothing hurts.'

JOE NAMATH
NFL QUARTERBACK

'Boxing brings out my aggressive instinct, not necessarily a killer instinct.'

SUGAR RAY LEONARD
WELTERWEIGHT BOXER

'When I was up there at the plate, my purpose was to get on base anyway I could, whether by hitting or by getting hit.'

SHOELESS JOE JACKSON
MLB OUTFIELDER

'I ain't the same person I was when I bit that guy's ear off.'

MIKE TYSON
HEAVYWEIGHT BOXER

'Tennis is a perfect combination of violent action taking place in an atmosphere of total tranquility.'

BILLIE JEAN KING
TENNIS PLAYER

'Every time I hear the name Joe Louis my nose starts to bleed.'

TOMMY FARR
HEAVYWEIGHT BOXER

'Sooner or later the arm goes bad. It has to. Sooner or later you have to start pitching in pain.'

WHITEY FORD
MLB PITCHER

'Wrestling is ballet with violence.'

JESSE VENTURA
WRESTLER AND POLITICIAN

'Playing goal is like being shot at.'

JACQUES PLANTE
NHL GOALIE

★ ★

'I bet some of you feel sorry for me. Well, don't. Having an artificial leg has its advantages. I've broken my right knee many times and it doesn't hurt a bit.'

TERRY FOX RUNNER

★ ★

'You can't dodge them all. I got hammered plenty of times through the years. But you just get up and keep playing. I can tell you from experience, though, sometimes it hurts like hell.'

TERRY BRADSHAW BROADCASTER AND NFL QUARTERBACK

★ ★

'I killed many a quarterback. I felt like I scored when I took their head off.'

HARVEY MARTIN
NFL DEFENSIVE END

'I try to catch them right on the tip of his nose, because I try to punch the bone into the brain.'

MIKE TYSON
HEAVYWEIGHT BOXER

'I wouldn't ever set out to hurt anyone deliberately unless it was, you know, important – like a league game or something.'

DICK BUTKUS
NFL LINEBACKER

'I've come to accept that the life of a frontrunner is a hard one, that he will suffer more injuries than most men and that many of these injuries will not be accidental.'

PELE
SOCCER FORWARD

195

'I don't think the discus will ever attract any interest until they let us start throwing them at each other.'

AL OERTER
DISCUS THROWER

'I've had just about everything punched. I've had things grabbed that just shouldn't be grabbed.'

TOM BRADY
NFL QUARTERBACK

'Football combines the two worst features of American life: violence and committee meetings.'

GEORGE WILL
COLUMNIST

'Usually when I wielded a hockey stick, it meant somebody was going to get hurt.'

STAN MIKITA
NHL RIGHT WINGER

'The base paths belonged to me, the runner. The rules gave me the right. I always went into a bag full speed, feet first. I had sharp spikes on my shoes. If the baseman stood where he had no business to be and got hurt, that was his fault.'

TY COBB MLB OUTFIELDER

WINNERS AND WINNING

'IF WINNING ISN'T EVERYTHING, WHY DO THEY KEEP SCORE?'
VINCE LOMBARDI NFL COACH

'Placing first is not the same as winning.'

ROGER EBERT
JOURNALIST AND CRITIC

'What are we out at the park for, except to win?'

LEO DUROCHER
MLB SHORTSTOP AND MANAGER

'Winners never quit and quitters never win.'

VINCE LOMBARDI
NFL COACH

'Imagination has a great deal to do with winning.'

MIKE KRZYZEWSKI
COLLEGE BASKETBALL COACH

'I celebrate a victory when I start walking off the field. By the time I get to the locker room, I'm done.'

TOM OSBORNE
COLLEGE FOOTBALL COACH AND POLITICIAN

'It's pitching, hitting and defense that wins. Any two can win. All three make you unbeatable.'

JOE GARAGIOLA MLB CATCHER AND BROADCASTER

★ ★

'Winning is overrated. The only time it is really important is in surgery and war.'

AL MCGUIRE
COLLEGE BASKETBALL COACH

'The secret to winning is constant, consistent management.'

TOM LANDRY
NFL CORNERBACK AND COACH

'I am a winner each and every time I go into the ring.'

GEORGE FOREMAN
HEAVYWEIGHT BOXER

'Any time you try to win everything, you must be willing to lose everything.'

LARRY CSONKA
NFL FULLBACK

'Winning isn't everything, but wanting it is.'

ARNOLD PALMER
GOLFER

'Never change a winning game; always change a losing one.'

BILL TILDEN
TENNIS PLAYER

'The win is more important than how you do it.'

KYLE JOHNSON
NFL FULLBACK

'Before you can win a game, you have to not lose it.'

CHUCK NOLL
NFL PLAYER AND COACH

'The trouble with referees is they don't care which side wins.'

TOM CANTERBURY
COLLEGE BASKETBALL PLAYER

'I think that the team that wins game five will win the series. Unless we lose game five.'

CHARLES BARKLEY
NBA POWER FORWARD

★ ★

'When we lost, I couldn't sleep at night. When we win, I can't sleep at night. But when you win, you wake up feeling better.'

JOE TORRE MLB PLAYER AND MANAGER

★ ★

'You can't win them all but you can try.'

BABE ZAHARIAS
TRACK AND FIELD ATHLETE

'To be great we need to win games we aren't supposed to win.'

JULIUS ERVING
NBA SMALL FORWARD

'I don't want to shoot my mouth in my foot, but those are games we can win.'

SHERMAN DOUGLAS
NBA POINT GUARD

'The winner ain't the one with the fastest car, it's the one who refuses to lose.'

DALE EARNHARDT
NASCAR DRIVER

'Better teams win more often than the teams that are not so good.'

TOM WATT
NHL COACH

'You've got to get to the stage in life where going for it is more important than winning or losing.'

ARTHUR ASHE TENNIS PLAYER

★ ★

'When you want to win a game, you have to teach. When you lose a game, you have to learn.'

TOM LANDRY NFL CORNERBACK AND COACH

★ ★

'A life of frustration is inevitable for any coach whose main enjoyment is winning.'

CHUCK NOLL
NFL PLAYER AND COACH

'He who has the fastest golf cart never has a bad lie.'

MICKEY MANTLE
MLB CENTER FIELDER

'A football team is like a beautiful woman. When you do not tell her, she forgets she is beautiful.'

ARSENE WENGER
SOCCER COACH

'The moment of victory is wonderful, but also sad. It means that your trip is ended.'

BILL TOOMEY
TRACK AND FIELD ATHLETE

'*Winning isn't getting ahead of others. It's getting ahead of yourself.*'

ROGER STAUBACH
NFL QUARTERBACK AND TEAM OWNER

'*What counts in sports is not the victory, but the magnificence of the struggle.*'

JOE PATERNO
COLLEGE FOOTBALL COACH

'*There are only two places in the league – first place and no place.*'

TOM SEAVER
MLB PITCHER

'*Winning isn't everything, it's the only thing.*'

VINCE LOMBARDI
NFL COACH

'*I've found you don't need to wear a necktie if you can hit.*'

TED WILLIAMS
MLB LEFTFIELDER

'Winners live in the present tense. People who come up short are consumed with future or past. I want to be living in the now.'

ALEX RODRIGUEZ MLB THIRD BASEMAN

WISDOM AND ADVICE

'WORK LIKE YOU DON'T NEED THE MONEY. LOVE LIKE YOU'VE NEVER BEEN HURT. DANCE LIKE NOBODY'S WATCHING.'
SATCHEL PAIGE MLB PITCHER

'You miss 100 percent of the shots you never take.'

WAYNE GRETZKY
NHL CENTER

'Service to others is the rent you pay for your room here on earth.'

MUHAMMAD ALI
HEAVYWEIGHT BOXER

'If you are going to throw a club, it is important to throw it ahead of you, down the fairway, so you don't have to waste energy going back to pick it up.'

TOMMY BOLT
GOLFER

'Make the present good, and the past will take care of itself.'

KNUTE ROCKNE
COLLEGE FOOTBALL COACH

'Never let your head hang down. Never give up and sit down and grieve. Find another way. And don't pray when it rains if you don't pray when the sun shines.'

SATCHEL PAIGE MLB PITCHER

★ ★

'If you travel first class, you think first class and you are more likely to play first class.'

RAYMOND FLOYD
GOLFER

'Don't ever forget that you play with your soul as well as your body.'

KAREEM ABDUL-JABBAR
NBA CENTER

'Play every game as if it is your last one.'

GUY LAFLEUR
NHL RIGHT WINGER

'Make the hard ones look easy and the easy ones look hard.'

WALTER HAGEN
GOLFER

'If you can't be on time, be early.'

JOHN WOODEN
COLLEGE BASKETBALL COACH

'As you walk down the fairway of life you must smell the roses, for you only get to play one round.'

BEN HOGAN
GOLFER

'Whatever you do, don't do it halfway.'

BOB BEAMON
TRACK AND FIELD ATHLETE

'Approach the game with no preset agendas and you'll probably come away surprised at your overall efforts.'

PHIL JACKSON
NBA COACH

'By the time you get to your ball, if you don't know what to do with it, try another sport.'

JULIUS BOROS
GOLFER

'If you want to surf, move to Hawaii. If you like to shop, move to New York. If you like acting and Hollywood, move to California. But if you like college football, move to Texas.'

RICKY WILIAMS NFL RUNNING BACK

'Never let the fear of striking out get in your way.'

BABE RUTH
MLB PITCHER AND OUTFIELDER

'Never make predictions, especially about the future.'

CASEY STENGEL
MLB OUTFIELDER AND
MANAGER

'Be brave if you lose and meek if you win.'

HARVEY PENICK
GOLFER

'Never break your putter and your driver in the same round or you're dead.'

TOMMY BOLT
GOLFER

'What you have to remember is that baseball isn't a week or a month but a season – and a season is a long time.'

CHUCK TANNER
MLB OUTFIELDER AND
MANAGER

'I would change policy, bring back natural grass and nickel beer. Baseball is the belly-button of our society. Straighten out baseball and you straighten out the rest of the world.'

BILL LEE MLB PITCHER

★ ★

'I remember when I was in college, people told me I couldn't play in the NBA. There's always somebody saying you can't do it, and those people have to be ignored.'

BILL CARTWRIGHT NBA CENTER AND COACH

★ ★

'You never ask why you've been fired because if you do, they're liable to tell you.'

JERRY COLEMAN
MLB SECOND BASEMAN AND BROADCASTER

'You've got to be very careful if you don't know where you're going, because you might not get there.'

YOGI BERRA
MLB PLAYER AND MANAGER

'Don't drink in the hotel bar, that's where I do my drinking.'

CASEY STENGEL
MLB OUTFIELDER AND MANAGER

'Swing hard, in case they throw the ball where you're swinging.'

DUKE SNIDER
MLB OUTFIELDER

'If you come to a fork in the road, take it.'

YOGI BERRA
MLB PLAYER AND MANAGER

'Strive for continuous improvement, instead of perfection.'

KIM COLLINS
TRACK AND FIELD ATHLETE

'Find the good. It's all around you. Find it, showcase it and you'll start believing in it.'

JESSE OWENS
TRACK AND FIELD ATHLETE

'Do your best when no one is looking. If you do that, then you can be successful in anything that you put your mind to.'

BOB COUSY
NBA POINT GUARD AND COACH

★ ★

'Happiness begins where selfishness ends. You cannot live a perfect day without doing something for someone who will never be able to repay you.'

JOHN WOODEN COLLEGE BASKETBALL COACH